It's a Buddy's World

by

Bud Gilham

authorHOUSE®

AuthorHouse™
1663 Liberty Drive, Suite 200
Bloomington, IN 47403
www.authorhouse.com
Phone: 1-800-839-8640

First published by AuthorHouse 9/29/2009

ISBN: 978-1-4343-7422-6 (e)
ISBN: 978-1-4343-7420-2 (sc)
ISBN: 978-1-4343-7421-9 (hc)

Library of Congress Control Number: 2008905521

Printed in the United States of America
Bloomington, Indiana

This book is printed on acid-free paper.

About Family Things

This part of the book is a collection of articles that I wrote about the adventures and misadventures of life as a parent, husband, and father. Life can be hard and sometimes very difficult, but I always looked for the positive. I hope I can transfer that feeling to you with this easy-reading, sometimes humorous outlook on family life. On a note of interest, these things did happen; reality is often stranger than fiction.

On a More Philosophical Note

The second section of this book deals with the more emotional and at times philosophical aspects or our living this life. In this section I have included articles that I have had published as well. It is not in any way what some people call an advice column, but I do hope it helps you to feel not all alone with your feelings, or brings a little understanding about some people's outlook on aspects of life.

In Answer to Your Child's Questions About Love

When I met my wife, we were both still in high school and were typical teenagers of the time: a little rebellious, fiercely independent, and of course we knew everything. Our first meeting we literally bumped into each other. I came around a corner and walked right into her, knocking her books to the floor. I remember picking them up, but my wife and I still differ on what I said. I maintain I said I was sorry; she maintains I said something about the intelligence of her gender and ethnic background. The next time I met my wife was at a school dance. After talking her into dancing and getting out on the floor, I immediately began to be a bit of a flirt. My wife is the only female who has ever slapped my face; it was a good hit, too. She informed me that she had come with someone else and that my behavior was not wanted by her. This had never happened to me before.

I loved riding my motorcycle, and even to this day love the feel of the wind, the motor, and the freedom to my soul. As a teenage girl, my future wife liked the idea of me being a bit of a rebel, but probably started to wonder about me when she observed my riding behavior. I used to cat walk my bike (ask someone who rides a bike), at times for several hundred meters. I used to be able to lay rubber in two gears and rather enjoyed the sound of those throaty pipes when they roared. At the old Brooks School, I used to ride my bike up and down those long cement stairs from the upper parking lot to the lower one. Hmm, maybe that is why my wife never liked riding with me. One thing led to another, as it usually does, and it was the day to pick her up for a real date. In retrospect, I understand now why my future mother-in-law was not that impressed with me for a while. I made the mistake of showing up at my future wife's home on my motorcycle. So there I was, resplendent in my faded denims, high black boots, dark glasses, long hair, cigarette pack in my pocket, black leather gloves, and cocky attitude. Not future son-in-law material. Being a typical teenager of the time, I did not think about first impressions to future family. Of course I was not thinking of marriage at that time either. My future wife was immediately told, "You are not going out with him!" She, being a typical teenage girl of the day, stated, "Watch me!" To make it short, we did not have a date that day; mothers are a fearsome lot. I never gave up my bike, but did begin to use the car when taking out my future wife. On our road to thirty-six years of marriage, we dated often during high school.

My next biggest blunder was bringing my wife home at 4 a.m. Not only were we in trouble for that, but somewhere during the course of the evening, we had lost her brother, who we were supposed to be looking after. My future father-in-law, after hearing our excuses, said only one short sentence, "Never again!" I always wondered if he meant being so late, or me seeing his daughter. My wife and I dated for almost two years. I graduated first and went off and joined the military. I came back on leave to visit her and found her all alone in her home. She was washing dishes, so I snuck up behind her, and slipped my hands under her arms, and placed them where I should not have. I woke up on her bed. Yes, she knocked me out cold, a good elbow smash to the bridge of my nose. My future wife and I were taking martial arts at the time; she has also knocked me out while sparring. I did the only thing I could after all this: I phoned her from 5,000 kilometers away and asked her to marry me Safety first. This year will be thirty-six years of marriage and almost forty of being in each other's life. So when my children asked that question, "How will I know it is the right one?" I just smile and say, "You will know."

Excuse Me, I Might
Have to Arrest You

Had to happen didn't it? I have been writing about events in my life, comedic relief I hope, and one of them was about the RCMP and me. So it stands to reason I must write about my wife and her encounters with the police. First, let me say that she was much better behaved, or smarter, than I was in her teenage years. As far as police went, she was a nonevent to them. But then she got married to me. Hmmmm, maybe I am the ingredient for slapstick not her. The first one was before we got married.

I have always, once I learned it that is, gone by the credo don't anger people in uniforms who carry guns and enforce the law. To me, my 1965 Ford Galaxy 500 convertible was the car of cars. I babied it and loved to have it sound like a real car. To this end I usually put blue bottle mufflers on it, or thrush. I had just purchased brand new mufflers, thrush this time, and was cruising around town. It was a beautiful summer day, so the top was down and the music was loud.

In the car were my soon-to-be wife, a buddy, and his soon-to-be wife (not certain if he knew this at the time). A police car pulled us over, and after the usual license and insurance, he got to it. "You sound like you need new mufflers." When I told him that they were brand new and the paint was not even off them yet, he looked under the car. "Thrush mufflers are illegal," he stated. Well folks, that's all it took. My soon-to-be wife tore into him like he was a combination of Attila the Hun and Jack the Ripper. Not only did she inform him that perhaps the establishment that sold them should be charged with a crime and not us, but she slid onto my side of the car to make her point. Furthermore, that just because we were all young people and the boys had long hair did not make us bad people. We like our music loud and that is not a crime either. At about this time, I looked at the policeman, who was looking at me, and we had one of those kinetic connections. "What have you gotten yourself into this time," I believe was the thought we shared. To his credit he tried to establish some kind of authority, but the little woman was having nothing to do with it. She had him on the ropes and continued to pummel him. My buddy and I lit up smokes and just listened. I was sure we would be spending the next day in a cell for some reason, when all of a sudden I heard those magic words, "Sorry to have bothered you folks. Have a nice day." Wow, we were not going to be Bubba's plaything for the evening after all. That was our first encounter with the RCMP as an almost couple. The rest, are hers alone.

After our marriage we purchased a ranch-style home. It was beautiful and included full plate window in the living room, with three small windows under it that opened for air circulation, etc. My wife, even in her early career, had some, well bad habits. Locking her keys in the house or car was a regular thing for a while. She had locked herself out of the house and was crawling in through one of those little windows, when a voice came from behind her, "Excuse me, is this your house?" The voice belonged to a patrolling RCMP constable. He probably thought he had just foiled a break-in. I should mention my dog had been washing my wife's face as she was trying to get into the house through the window. My wife explained this point to the policeman: "The dog thinks I belong here." She had to crawl in, get her identification, and come to the front door, the policeman watching all the time. OK, she didn't get arrested for a B&E. Yep, you guessed it, round two. Again with the keys securely locked in the house, she was doing the window thing once more. Yes, the same scene played out, but different policeman. (I wonder if they were still following me from my youth, hmmmm.) The outcome was a smiling policeman shaking his head, wife not arrested (face washed by dog for second time). Oh ya, round three came along, same scenario, same window, same bottom trying to wiggle through it. This is where it changed this time. A horn sounded behind her, and she turned around to see a police car. The smiling policemen just waved. "Locked yourself out again, ma'am?" they asked. To her credit she said nothing, just nodded her head and went back to the face washing by my dog, and the journey in through the now getting smaller windows (found out she was pregnant at about this time). Now, onto my wife the counterfeiter, hee hee.

Like most guys, I often forget to empty my pockets when putting my clothes into the washing. (I dare anyone to say you never have. Yes, a Kleenex counts.) My wife went along doing the washing, and when she opened the washing machine, well what a surprise. I had left my entire paycheck, in $20 bills, in one of my pant pockets. The wife, being the clear thinker that she is, shrugged her shoulders, took out the wet money and clothes, and put in the next load. Tossing the clothes into the dryer, less the sopping money, she turned on the machines and looked at the wet currency. Again, with clear thinking, she decided to hang it out to dry. Knowing it was money, she strung a couple lines inside the basement, actually the basement windows as the sun was shining in through them. With the clothes drying, she hung up our money. The dryer ended its cycle, she put in the wet sneakers to dry, and went back to her money laundering. As she was blissfully hanging our new money, a screech of tires sounded in front of the house. My wife saw nothing so continued on with her task. Soon a rapping came to the window. "Good day, ma'am," the policeman, who was thinking *Oh boy a good bust*, said. When he asked what she was doing with the money, she said drying it because it was still wet. (Hmmm, maybe the wrong wording at the time, dear). Behind her was the regular clunk, clunk sound of the sneakers in the dryer. Combined with the money hanging, and yes it does sound the same, the policeman thought, *Wet money … printing press in other room … counterfeiter*. Postscript to thought pattern: Not very bright counterfeiter. The officer made my wife come to the door; he searched the house and examined the money. He believed her story, obviously a married man who has done the "leave in the pocket" thing, too.

To my knowledge, that was the last police incident involving my wife. I think they talked, and somewhere there is a file on her, maybe not flattering, but at least not criminal. Since these incidents, I would like to point out that we have had several interactions with the local RCMP. I wonder why they smile so much around us. Oh well, life goes on and so must I. Until the next installment of, whatever this is, take care people and remember to laugh.

Ahh Yes, Raising Children

The idea for this little piece came from reading an article submitted by a mother to a paper. It described the various antics of her offspring and a ceiling fan. (One of mine did the same thing, only they were older and should have known better.) It made me realize all the things that happen when you do not have a camera around. Without proof, would they believe you? Oh yes, just look at the parents nodding their heads. The perils of parenthood, in comic relief.

The day I saw my firstborn is a day etched permanently in my memory. Alongside of this is the first time I saw my second and third children. I had wanted to be a father since I was sixteen, to be part of creating a new life. The way their little bright eyes would sparkle when you talked to them or made funny noises is so pure and innocent. The room would fill with their little laughs, giggles, gurgles, and other noises, and life was good. Then it happened. They began to move.

As new parents, we discovered quickly how fast these little creatures called children can be. While changing one of them (can't remember which), the baby rolled and I caught him or her, as they rolled off the counter. OK, on the floor from now on, or one hand on baby tummy at all times. Have you ever noticed that children never come with how-to instructions? The next stage, of course, is when they discover they can get up on their hands and knees. At first it is cute; they are there rocking back and forth, ahhh so cute. No, next it is the monster crawler scenario. The devil soon discovers just how fast they can motor across the room. Oh and look, there is stuff on the floor over there, like electrical cords. OK, new safety arrangements for house; plugs will be covered and all electrical and sharp thingies are made safe or removed. Soon they discover they can crawl up things, like furniture or walls. My daughter had this one down. She would crawl like mad across the room, up the side of the couch to the standing position, and wait. The family dog would wonder by, minding its own business, and she would pounce. To the dog's credit, this became a game for it, too. It would come close to the child after she had gotten back up and wait just out of reach, then dart past as my daughter made the lunge; she missed. The two of them would spend hours playing this game, her giggling and dog just wagging its tail and, if it could, laughing to itself. This is, of course, the stage of child development where parents find new and better ways to keep cupboard doors fastened. The first time one of the children opened the cupboard and took out the entire inventory of pots and pans was deafening. Oh yes, and of course the famous gates at the top of all stairs, hell for short-legged people like me to step over (ahhh ouchy). Then on one miraculous day, they do it. They stand on their own and begin to walk. Oh God, now they are really mobile.

It seems like only a matter of weeks from their first step to pushing and climbing on chairs to reach things in higher places. Note: higher cupboard doors now require fastening, all things off counter, knives and cooking utensils moved to safer locations, end of note. Of course now chains or other hard-to-open locking devices must be installed on all outside doors. These security chains were not originally designed to keep people out, but the little people from getting out and exploring the world on their own. As the growth and mobility continue, parents find themselves in a constant state of rearranging their possessions and memorabilia to higher, safer locations. The first time you see one of your children after they have found mother's makeup is a sight to see. Thank goodness none of it was poisonous. We knew the next stage was upon us when one of my sons took runs at the gates at the top of the stairs, trying to break out of the home I guess. I realize he liked the way it would bend and spring back, sending him sprawling on the floor. But he did not know his own strength and, to our horror, actually smashed through it on one occasion. As we ran down the stairs, hearts in mouths, the little rat was giggling like crazy at the bottom of the stairs. Thank goodness these little creatures seem to come with some kind of indestructible shield. Now more than just one floor of the house had to be childproofed, if you can ever accomplish such a thing.

Of course more things now begin to happen; they do come with brains that are just full of curiosity. What happens to my brother when I run over his arm with my tricycle? That was one we did get on camera. Then there was the one when two of them decided to bathe their very quiet brother in cornstarch and oatmeal (don't ask). By now they are making regular ventures into the backyard; oh boy a whole new set of dangers. "Yes Son, I do remember you painting my nice convertible with wood stain! And the time I was working under my Land Rover in the snow and you decided to pile snow around the vehicle to keep me warm." I believe all three were in on that one. This is the time when I believe my hair began to turn gray very fast. The first time they ride their two-wheeler and then go to school. The first time they discover how far they can throw things, such as rocks. The first time they discover the sound of breaking glass from said projectile. The first time you see your child racing down your driveway on their two-wheeler and right toward the plank they had set up as a jump. My real wake-up call came the day my wife came home with our daughter's first bra. What? No way, she is not old enough yet! I think that was about the time gun collecting became my hobby. Of course my sons were also reaching that age of, oh God, TEENAGERS! Ahhhhhhhhhgggg, more gray hairs, ulcers, heart palpitations. How did this happen? Have you noticed how fast those years went by? I mean from holding this little bright-eyed cute baby to training bra! Wow, that was fast!

Children do not come with operating instructions, and parents, we don't have how-to manuals. Over the years, our family survived with many good times. We had snowball fights, water fights, played all kinds of games of soccer, street hockey, board games, and so on. There were, of course the "I have to be the parent" days: groundings for misdeeds, bedtimes and the accompanying games of drinks of water and sneaking out of bedroom. But we laughed far more than we did not. That's the secret I guess. So many Christmas days of absolute joy and pleasure in watching their faces and playing with their toys (I still love Tonka brand trucks). Oh yes, and the one with the Soccer Boppers. The great foods, the great birthday parties, the great times are there. They outweigh the worry we have over our children. Did we teach them all the right things? Did we prepare them for life? After they leave home, are they being careful? Are they OK, are they looking after themselves? Mom, Dad, you did good, don't worry. Anyone who can have children, raise them to the time they become adults, and everyone survives, is a genius. The real reward for my wife and me is that they still call and still visit. They still ask us and talk to us about things in their lives. We still laugh and have fun together as a family. To my children, I say thank you. You are what made my life and your mother's so rich. Each day we smile and feel the warmth of the love that created you, raised you, and nurtured you and us. We are very proud of you all and love you with all of our being. Oh ya, just in case you were wondering about moving back home, your mother and I are moving ... we will write. And those children you now have, our grandchildren, it's called payback. Enjoy!

My Attempt at Farming

I was asked to write another short article about summer, or something close to it. Well, I wanted to avoid this topic, but the editor found a source who talked freely. So, here you go folks, a short journey into the world of getting back to the land, by someone who should not have made the trip.

I was fortunate to be the offspring of farm folk. We never wanted for fresh fruits, vegetables, or meat. My parents cultivated a large garden and a small orchard, and my father was good at hunting and fishing. My mother was very adept at canning and preserving the vegetables and fruits, so over the winter we enjoyed them as well. Probably because of the work I had to do when growing up, I never really caught on to the farming idea. The concept was great—I love fresh fruits and vegetables—but the reality was somewhat less appealing. I did not like the amount of time and effort I had to put into pruning trees, raking leaves, cultivating large gardens by hand, and spreading manure, seaweed, and lime over the gardens and orchards. The amount of hours spent preparing the soil and maintaining its fertility was not my idea of how to spend time. Let's face it, what teenager would? I grew older, not wiser, and got married. Just kidding, dear.

As is the way of things, after marriage came children. I had a good-paying job and we never suffered for lack of anything, but as parents we became concerned about what we were eating. Yes, the wife and I like A&W, Kentucky Fried Chicken, and Chinese takeout, right along with the kids. To rectify the apparent debauchery that was assailing our good health, it was decided we should have a garden. Uh oh. Well, first I had to build a fence for the garden, right, then stain it, and of course I had to build the garden shed to hold the tools, manure, etc. Jeez, no garden, the soil had not even been turned, and I had a summer of work to do. I still don't quite remember me getting a vote on this particular adventure; oh well on with the story. Like a dutiful husband, I constructed the necessary buildings and fencing, then turned the soil in preparation for planting (I used a rototiller). We planted our garden, tended it, and harvested a fine crop. We did this for a couple of years, then realized two things. One, we did not have much time to spend having fun with the children (that was my excuse, folks). Second, we could buy fresh vegetables or fruits from vendors who brought it to Powell River to sell at very reasonable prices. So, we could buy it and can it or preserve it without the back-breaking, sun-baked toil of growing it. Case closed, and so was the garden. This was fine until someone decided we could raise our own meat. So the fenced-in area and shed now became part of our pig farm (well, OK just two pigs).

This enterprise—again I don't remember my voting stance on this issue—went along quite well actually. We got fresh vegetables and fruits from local stores, the stuff they have to throw out because of age or damage. That, along with the grain, shots, and other pig dietary concerns produced two very large and tasty looking porkers. So, what happened to close down this enterprise you are asking yourself. Hee hee. Well, a few things hastened the end of pig farming and the pigs.

First, let me say that raising pigs, especially with inadequate fencing, is problematic. The porkers could soon push over or go under my fence and roam the backyard and the neighbor's. Fence repair and pig round up became commonplace. Note: when pig farming, use rail fencing, not the slat type. End of note. There was the time my son was feeding them and they got overzealous and bit off part of his boot. That was the end of his pig farming, as expressed in a very eloquent speech to us with a lot of, "No bloody way," and, "They have huge teeth," phrases. Well, so far it was becoming a problem, but manageable. Then the little porkers did something all us men know not to do. *Don't upset the woman of the house!* It happened on an evening when the wife and I were heading out for a special evening. She had on her nice long gown and I had on a suit and tie. Then it started. "Mom, Dad the pigs got out again!" Yep, you know the first word out of my mouth don't you?

Well, while the children herded the porkers around, the wife and I donned coveralls over our finery and then joined the fray. We got them back into the pen and then noticed where they had pushed under the fence. By now I had several logs around to cover such emergencies. I explained to the wife we would just place one and secure it for now, then be on our way. We retrieved a suitable sized log and began to carry it toward the broken part of the fence. Oh, for those of you that don't know, pigs like to dig very large holes. Hee hee. My wife, for reasons known only to her, decided to walk backward. First mistake. I tried to warn her, but too late. She fell into one of the larger holes the pigs had created. I, of course, knew I would not be able to hold onto the log. I was concerned that as my wife fell, the log would come down and strike her on the chest or abdomen. So I yelled for her to let go and tossed the log away from me as she fell. Not away from us, folks, away from me. My wife ended up in the hole, arms and legs sticking out, held firmly in place by the log lying across the hole and her stomach. The log did not hit her and she was not hurt, but she was firmly pinned and now the fun started. Pigs figure anything down in their pigpen is food. This is the picture: wife on back like stuck crab, pigs zeroing in on feet as appetizers, husband standing looking at scene. I could not help it, folks. Between my wife's flailing around and the pigs' apparent confusion as to why their food was moving, I started to laugh. While she kicked and cussed out the pigs in two languages, I tried to lift the log off her and kick at the pig that had decided I was lunch as well. It took what seemed like forever, but I freed her and we got out of the pen. Only my wife's pride was injured. But as we secured the gate behind us, she glared at the pigs and told me to call our friend, the man who was going to help us slaughter the pigs. So much for a long and happy life guys.

As you can see, I may come from good farm stock, but I am no farmer. My wife and I have since been supermarket farmers. I truly admire those who can cultivate good gardens and orchards and raise farm animals. I truly understand how much time and effort you put into it. But I am not one of those people. I can understand fishing and hunting; those I can do. Farming? Sorry, I would be a plague worse than locust as a farmer. And you know what? A&W, Kentucky Fried Chicken, and Chinese takeout are not all that bad. See you in the fast-food lineup.

That Good Old
Summer Time (Uh Huh)

"Those Lazy, Hazy, Crazy Days of Summer," or how about, "In the Good Old Summertime"? Ah yes, many songs have been written about summer. My favorites were "Schools Out for the Summer," or "We're Not Gonna Take It Anymore." The rebel in me, right? I was just pondering my keyboard here, wondering what I could write about summer. I, of course, want it to be light and bring a smile to the faces of those who read this. Camping tales from my youth would be filled with stories of hardship, danger, and near-death experiences. I was camping and backpacking when I was nine years old. This was long before it became vogue and the market was flooded with designer everything for the outdoorsman. Sorry, my idea of being in the wilderness was being in the wilderness. I carried one pack with everything in it, slept in shelters built by me for the night, and usually did not see another human being. By the time I was a family man, I had been camped out so to speak. Besides, my children were precious to me, and I would not put them in situations like those I

21

had as a youth. We did go camping, of course, and fishing and four-wheeling. I thought rather than one tale, I would relate some things I observed and experienced as a father and husband. Hee, hee, here we go, family, you all get it this time.

There was the time I got the truck stuck in the mud. While I was using the jack and pieces of wood to get us unstuck, my lovely little daughter was aiding the cause. As I was busy working and trying not to use colorful metaphors, "#@*"(like those), my daughter was very busy as well. With the skill and patience of a pro thief, she was gently pouring soft white sand down the back of my pants. My dutiful wife was standing there observing all this, hand clamped firmly over her mouth of course. Folks, standing up to find almost a kilogram or two of gritty sand in the nether regions of your clothing is an experience, let me tell you. I looked down into the innocent face of my daughter. She had a huge smile that of course melted my heart, plus her small hand held more of the evidence of her deed. My wife almost had to cross her legs she was holding back the giggles so much. What could I do? I just laughed and thanked my daughter for being such a good helper. OK, on to my next victim.

My oldest son was quite small when he was a child. While he was young, he had an experience that caused me a few gray hairs. I had built a beautiful and large sundeck on our home, and we enjoyed it quite often. I even played soccer with the kids on the deck. I was helping the wife set up the patio furniture on the deck; it was a beautiful hot and windy day. Remember the "windy," folks. I had opened the table umbrella, but the wife was having trouble with the table, so I asked my oldest boy to hold onto the umbrella while I helped his mother. My wife looked up for some reason and yelled out our son's name. I turned to see him being gently lifted off the deck. I told him to hang onto the umbrella as I ran toward him. Too late. The wind picked him up off the deck, over the four-foot railing around the deck, and off toward our backyard. I vaulted over the rail and clambered down the support posts of the deck, while watching our son floating away. He made it about ten or twenty meters before the wind gently lowered him to the lawn in our backyard. My son never said a word, just handed me the umbrella when I reached him. He probably wonders to this day why his father hugged him so hard. Yep, my son tried to be Mary Poppins and succeeded. OK, son number two, it is your turn now.

Son number two is the hardest to describe, and the easiest. He inherited traits from both of his parents, like his siblings of course, but certain ones he seemed to get an overdose of. He seemed to inherit my adventurous spirit and his mother's often incredible tendency for getting into some kind of, shall we say ... situation. For me, the fortunate thing is he gave his mother more gray hairs than he did me. His adventures seemed to happen when Dad was not there. Our homes have always had large yards and lots of forest around. One summer day, one of the other children came in to tell their mother the youngest son had climbed a tree. When my wife did not seem to get too upset at the statement, our child insisted their mother go out onto the sundeck and have a look. My wife strolled out to see our youngest boy gleefully swaying back and forth to his heart's content at the top of a tree. Not just any tree, folks, a very tall cedar tree. Now I am lousy at guessing the height of trees and such, let's just say it was at least high enough to scare the you know what out of my wife. What do you think she said? Yep, "You get down out of that tree right now," she yelled at him. Our little daredevil obliged by letting go and dropping to the next branch. He continued this decent all the way down to the bottom. There he met my wife, his mother, and after ensuring he was OK, she gave him the biggest lecture of his young life. He probably never understood why until years later, when he realized it was fear: he had scared his mother to death. Now on to the queen of slapstick. Heee, heee. Oh, I could write a book on the misadventures of the wife with bears and fishing. But, unless I wish to spend the rest of my life in China, alone, I had best pick a not-so-bad one, right?

I had taken the family high into the mountains, to a lake that was very pretty and had some good fishing. My wife had been fishing with me many times for salmon, cod, red snapper, and trout. She had never done casting; we had always trolled or jigged. I took her to the edge of the lake and instructed her on how to hold and release the brake during the casting motion. I warned her about making sure no one was near; you don't want to hook something other than a fish. I stood out of the way and watched her as she drew back the rod, pushed the button, and sent the lure arching out toward the placid lake. The lure, the line, and the rod. I just watched in dumfounded disbelief as my casting rod sailed out over the lake and shattered the placid surface of the water as it plummeted to the lake bottom. Our children were next to me, and one of them uttered, "Is that supposed to happen?" My wife just stood there, looking at the lake for a few minutes, then turned and looked at us. "I think I was supposed to hang onto the rod," she said softly. I just nodded my head and told her that would have been a good idea. She had been concentrating so hard on performing a good cast, and so marveled at the fact that she did one, that she had let go of the rod in her excitement. Oh well, I just stripped down and went diving. Yes, I did get the rod back, folks.

I could fill many pages with the often silly things that happen in ordinary family life, but that is enough for now. After all, I may not be able to show my face to my family as it is. If you have ever had the pleasure of listening to Bill Cosby comedy records, you will begin to understand. In the average everyday life of being a parent or husband, there are enough little situations to make a career comedy-rich with material. This type of humor is not malicious, mean, prejudicial, or rampant with foul language and sexual overtones. It is the ordinary things ordinary people do in their ordinary lives. If we can't laugh at ourselves, how can we ever share love and gentleness with others? If you can't laugh at the world sometimes, it gets depressing enough to chew you up and spit you out. So laugh, folks, remember those times that bring a smile to your face and a glow in your heart. Those are more precious than anything else in our lives. So long for now.

Motorcycles and Me

As the weather gets warmer, I of course reminisce about the summers of my youth. Some of those summers, and winters, were spent riding a motorcycle. I really can't describe the feeling you get when you crack that throttle and feel the power of a good bike. The sense of freedom as you travel down highways, seeing much more than you do from any other vehicle. I found city traffic was the only thing I did not like when on my bike. I had only my legs out there, no metal around them for added protection.

My bike riding experiences are probably like most other riders have had. The bee that gets into your helmet (that's when you find out how fast you can stop a bike and get that helmet off). On one trip I picked up a hitchhiker (a pigeon that sat on the back of my bike for several hundred kilometers). There was the time I got caught in a snowstorm (riding a motorcycle in almost whiteout conditions gives a whole new meaning to "Holy shit"). There were, of course, the times you had a person on the back and they just would not lean the right way. This makes it very hard to maneuver a bike around corners at high speed. I also had many close calls on my bike, some were not accidental either. It seems some people think it is fun to scare motorcyclists by getting really, really close. I had one fine citizen force me off the road into a ditch, and another who forced me into oncoming traffic. When a car ran a red light and hit me, sending my bike and me sailing through an intersection, I was beginning to lose the lust for riding. Don't get me wrong, I did not stop riding motorcycles, or lose the thrill of riding them, I just starting thinking about other drivers and their motives a little more. I realized my naïveté: some people just don't like motorcycles or those who ride them. At the time I was riding, motorcycle gangs were the big things in Hollywood movies, so of course anyone on a bike was a biker. Right, like my BSA resembled a hog (that's a cut-down Harley, folks, also called a chopper). Not to mention the fact that a lot of us who rode bikes did not wear leather and did not display any colors (motorcycle club insignias such as Hells Angles). I also knew some who did belong to bike gangs, and they were not bad people. Of course that was a while ago; my time was when Powell River's own 101 Knights was the club of the coast. I eventually sold my bike and went the car route, until years later when, yep you guessed it, THE WIFE.

I had never been able to get my wife to ride with me, but a couple years into our marriage she thought a small bike might be good for riding in the bush. May the God of motorcycles forgive me, she wanted a Honda 90. Being stubborn, or afraid to ride with me, she decided to teach herself. I finally convinced her that keeping the throttle wide open was not the only way to stay up on a bike. Anyway, one day she made a fatal mistake: she allowed me to drive and she climbed on the back (hee, hee, hee). Now I was a good boy, no cat walking, no high-speed, low-banked turns, and no ripping down the straight stretches of road. I had taken her to some old roads and trails that were pretty smooth and had great scenery. We were cruising along, everything was going fine, and then it happened. The trail we were on began to have little dips and rises in it, and they were rolling ones, spaced just right. You got this real great rush as you went down, then up and over the top, and I do mean over; a little airtime was involved as the bike left the ground. To my delight, the wife actually started to enjoy this rather more adventurous riding style. We went over one rise that was quite good; the bike got real good airtime. I turned to say something intelligent like, "wow," and she was gone. I mean she was gone, folks, not on the bike and not on the trail behind. I spun the bike around and looked down the trail. Nope, no wife. I cut the engine and called her name; I heard this voice calling out to me and began to move back the way we had come. I looked in the bush at the side of the trail as I slowly rode along. I hear this, "Hey, over here!" I stopped the bike and cut the engine, but could not see her. "Up here!" I looked up from ground level, where you expect to find someone who has fallen off a bike, and there she was, part way up a tree. The trail we had been on had tree branches that stretched out onto it. When I had gained airtime on the last little rise, one of those tree branches had somehow gone right into the belt loop of her pants as the bike left the ground. The effect was a slingshot motion that took her off the back of the bike as we were coming back down to earth. She must have left the bike while we were in the air, because I had felt no movement or weight change. I am happy to say that it did not deter my wife from riding, and she did eventually learn how to handle a bike quite well. Unfortunately, she ran into those who like to walk their dogs off the leash. After a few encounters with leg biters and owners who were not responsible enough to keep their dogs under control, and of course blamed the bike rider for upsetting their good little doggy, she stopped riding. She told me that she was beginning to feel like riding down the owners after kicking off their good little doggies. I nodded my head; in my youth, more than one car had been kicked by me when it tried to run me off the road. I guess some things just never change. Some people think anyone who rides a bike has to be a troublemaker or some other such anomaly. Hold that thought the next time you see grandmothers and grandfathers touring around in clubs. You know the type: the geriatric hoodlums. The price of freedom is often scorned by those who have never had it, or are afraid to try it. So happy riding to all those bike riders who still straddle the saddle. My heart and soul are with you as the wind tightens your face muscles. Oh ya, keep the mouth closed: them bees just are nasty sometimes aren't they?

Starting to Feel Like Christmas

Well, well, well, it is that time of the year again. No, not tax time, but it will be with us soon. Christmas is almost upon us again. Christmas, where does the time go? When I was a child it, was the most joyous of times for me; I could hardly sleep for days before Christmas Eve. On the blessed morning, I would open my stocking, one of my father's large wool work socks (I was not a stupid child, ha, ha). I would open my small prizes, eat the mandarin oranges and candies and wait impatiently for the family to wake up. I would creep out and ogle all the wrapped gifts under the tree and try to imagine their contents. The air almost seemed alive with a strange feeling of excitement and peace, a very strange combination when you think on it. As the years rolled by, I became older, and a more mature attitude toward the day crept in, damned shame that. There were the gifts, the dinners, the visits, but it did not hold the same magic for me. Then I met my future wife, and she would spend part of the day at my parents' home, then I at her parents' home. The magic came back.

After we were married and had our own home, Christmas days and the magic of my youth returned with the birth of each child. As the children grew, it got better and better. I could again play with the toys from under the tree, laugh and roll on the floor with childlike abandonment. Ah, Christmas it was, and is, a most wondrous day. Of course it is the spirit of this day that we try to keep with us all year, and many of us do try. Many a Christmas have rolled by now, and the children come to our home or we go to theirs for dinner. My wife and I have one grandson who lives with us, so we still have a good Christmas morning experience. But more and more, my wife and I reminisce about past Christmases. This memory lane journey never fails to bring a smile or a chuckle to us; we have had many great Christmas days in our family.

There were a few times when we actually had enough snow to build snow forts and snowmen and have snowball fights. When we did not have enough snow, we would pile into my Land Rover and head for the mountains. There we could tube down a road and play in the snow. My children used to tell me to stop going for walks in the snow before Christmas if we had any; when I did, it always seemed to rain on Christmas Day. The most fun was, of course, Christmas Day itself.

There was the time we bought all the children dart guns. You remember, the ones that used to shoot those rubber suction cups that would stick to Mom's nice clean walls and appliances. Also your brother's forehead. Unknown to them, my wife and I had bought one for each of us as well. So on Christmas morning, as our children tried to sneak into our bedroom with their planned terrorist attack, Mother and I sat up and opened fire. Well the squeals screams and sounds of spring-released projectiles filled the air. For hours that day, the war of the dart guns waged. My oldest boy did not fare well. I am not a mean or stupid father, but no matter where I aimed my dart gun, he seemed to somehow move into the path of the dart. And every time the little rubber suction cup would strike and affix itself to the lens of his glasses. Honest, folks, I am not that good of a shot. I even tried to aim at his younger brother; nope, the glasses again. What can I say? It was a kind of weird Christmas magic. And then there was the year of the Christmas ghost tree.

As usual, we had trimmed the tree, an entire family event. Another tradition in our house is to watch Charles Dickens's *A Christmas Carol*, (*Scrooge*), on Christmas Eve. Anyway, I had noticed that every day, my wife or I were picking up Christmas bulbs that had fallen from the tree. We just figured they were getting old and the hooks were not as good anymore. On Christmas Eve, we were watching *Scrooge*, when one of my young children grabbed my arm. I patted their hand and reminded them it is only a movie. My child whispered, "The tree is moving!" I looked at the Christmas tree but saw no movement. A short time later, my wife stated, "The tree is moving." Yep, when I looked, it was swaying back and forth. Slowly I got up and approached the now bewitched symbol of Christmas. My children were huddled around their mother, eyes wide, mouths open. I was just about to touch the tree when my heart jumped. From under a string of blue garland, a white and gray face appeared. "Smokey!" I exclaimed. Then a bulb fell down at my feet. Looking upward, I saw the black and white face of Smokey's brother, Satan. Yep, for the last several days, our two little kittens had been quietly exploring the Christmas tree. That explained the fallen bulbs and ended the mystery of the ghost in the Christmas tree.

Over the years, our various pets have been a source of amusement around Christmas. They always seem to want to investigate and sleep in, on, or around the Christmas tree and gifts. And when it snowed, well that was a new set of events to see. Have you ever seen a cat when it first steps into that white stuff, you know snow? They lift up their paw, look at it, look at you as if to say, "What the @#%& is this stuff!" They bravely leap out, to disappear, only the tail visible. Then they begin to leap, disappear, leap, and disappear in a vain attempt to move through the snow with some form of dignity. One of our dogs, for some strange reason, used to put its nose down into the snow and then run like hell all over the yard. Guess he thought he was a snowplow.

There are many other strange and wonderful things that happened over the years, but this article is getting long enough for the editor. So, I hope you all get yet another day of wonderful memories, good food, and good company. Merry Christmas to you all, and have a Happy New Year from a guy in China. Hmm, wonder if they have turkeys here. Doesn't matter: no ovens to cook them in anyway. So long for now.

Father's Day

Ahh, the month of June. Graduations, weddings, the start of summer, and Father's Day. I am glad that someone somewhere decided to dedicate a day to fathers. The only question I had was Why June? Think about it. What do weddings, graduations, and the beginning of summer have in common with Father's Day? Well, let's see.

Graduation is a ceremony to signify the completion of something, usually some sort of training or education process. (Never mind the smart comments, ladies.) It also signifies, to some of us, moving on to the next phase in one's life. High school graduation is usually full of speeches about new beginnings, new hopes, shaping the future, and of course, good luck and good wishes. How could I tie this in with Father's Day? Well, as a father you have been part of the creation of new life. You have definitely moved on to a new phase in your life; they call it parenthood (read my article on raising children to refresh your memory). Your child, or children, represent a new beginning, new hopes, and we all hope our children have a good life and do better than we did (why, I am not quite sure; I think I did OK). I know, I know, we hope they won't make the mistakes we did. Don't worry; they will come up with new ones for you. OK, so Father's Day is a kind of reminder of our graduation from being a husband to becoming a father. We even celebrate the blessed event of newborns with parties, best wishes, good luck, well done, and cigars. Not sure where the cigar one came from. So Father's Day is the remembering of our graduation to being a parent. What about weddings?

Weddings, in most cultures, are a ceremony where a man and a woman publicly declare their love for each other and dedication to building a future life together. It is, I suppose, a kind of graduation as well. We graduate from the simple life of a single person to the complicated, often turbulent life of being part of a couple. We (men), give up or lose something. It is like giving up your teenage years and moving into adulthood. (Hmmm, maybe not a good comparison. I can hear the comments, ladies.) But weddings traditionally celebrate love, devotion, and all the higher virtues we aspire to. As a father, we celebrate love and devotion and all those higher virtues in our children. We love our child or children, and hope we can guide them through the early years of life to a good future. We try to teach them what we see as good, and how to avoid the bad things in this world. We aspire to give them the skills to survive, to be a good person, and to find love. What about the joining together aspect of the wedding ceremony? Well, as fathers we have joined in the creation of new life, of creating part of the future generations, and there is a bonding between fathers and their children. OK, sometimes this bonding is like two pieces of sandpaper, but we bond. We are connected to our children for the rest of our lives. As the words in most wedding ceremonies state, "Until death do us part." Or, as I say to my children,

"No matter what happens, what you do or become, I will always be your father." OK, so Father's Day is like the wedding anniversary? Is it a reminder of the day we joined in creating our children? I think it is the day to remind us of the love, pride, and joy we felt the day we held our newborn child. The day we remember what being a father is really all about. What about the beginning of summer?

This one is a little tricky. In the cycle of life, many writers refer to spring as your youth and summer as the years of love and highest productivity or most life events. Summer usually signifies warmth, growing, and all the positive things of life; in general, it's a good time. OK, so how does this one work in with Father's Day? Hmmm, let me think a moment. Well, as a father, you are usually not considered a youth anymore. Once you have become a father, you tend to become more productive (in making a living, guys). We tend to settle down to a life of raising our children, maintaining a home, seeing to our offspring's formal education, and of course, all the presents we give them. My time with my children as we raised them was happy, warm, and exciting. Sometimes more exciting than I would have it, but hey that's life. So OK, it is like the beginning of summer. Being a father is the zenith of our life cycle; it is the time when we are most alive, display our emotions, are filled with pride, hope, all the nice things. It is a time of warmth, love, and probably the beginning of the busiest part of our life span. Unlike the seasons, fatherhood does not wane in the fall or the winter cycle of our lifetime. It just changes like the seasons. In the fall of our lives we sometimes get to see the harvest, if you like. Our children grow to adulthood and have children of their own perhaps. We become the dreaded grandparents. We tend to start slowing down a little and just enjoy the fruits of our labor, so to speak. We revel in our grandchildren; we spoil them (then send them home to terrorize their parents). In the winter of our lives, we can even sometimes see great-grandchildren, and we hope this family we helped create is strong with the virtues we held high: love, dedication, compassion, and understanding. Our children and grandchildren will now reverse roles and help ease our lives as we close out our seasons. Or as my son stated, "Don't worry. I'll give your wheelchair a good push down that hill." So, like the beginning of summer, Father's Day celebrates all the good things in our life.

That is my take on Father's Day, folks. Remember, life is better with more smiles and laughter than tears and sorrow. Sometimes we have to work at that part, or get help from someone to aid us through the rough spots. My children have done that for me; I only hope I have been able to do the same for them. Thank you to my children for still remembering who I am (the old guy who used to be young). You know the guy who used to give you the car, money, presents. YOUR FATHER, DAMMIT! Oops, sorry folks. I hope this brought a smile or two to your face and your heart. Take care until the next article, and happy Father's Day.

Summer: A Bear Able Season

One of the constants of summer is the encounters between humans and bears. In Powell River, you don't even have to leave home for it to happen. I have watched as black bears gleefully destroy the neighbor's fruit tree or garden. I have seen them sniffing around my woodshed or pond. I got upset with the one that wanted to den up under my woodshed, and there was the one that decided one of my dogs would be a good meal. I think the bear is a magnificent creature, and I respect their power and hunting abilities. I never realized that bears could be such a large part of comedic encounters though. That was not until they met my wife. (I really am going to have to stop telling these tales or I might end up in divorce court, folks.)

My wife and I both were brought up with access to forests and lakes. (Maybe that explains why we are how we are.) Anyway, my wife was a regular *courier de bois* when she was a young girl. She could trap, fish, and hunt with the best of them. In fact, after she and I met, I had to make several trips to where she was camping with her family; they were and are real lovers of the outdoors. This love of the outdoors did not change after we got married; we four-wheeled, camped, and hiked most of the area around Powell River. I find it very strange that our most memorable encounters with bears happened on our own property.

The first tale happened on a warm summer afternoon. We had been doing something with tomatoes, as the wife was taking the bad ones to the compost. As she walked across the back lawn, our dogs began to bark insistently. My wife, thinking they were just barking because they wanted out to play, told them to be quiet. She reached the compost, and the dogs were almost coming over their fence and barking. The wife, realizing this was unusual behavior, looked around. Coming toward her at a run was a black bear. My wife threw a tomato at the bear and ran for the back of the house. She literally ran out of her sandals, cleared a three-foot cement wall, and made it to the back door. During this dash, she was throwing tomatoes over her shoulder at the pursuing bear. All ended well: wife was safe, dogs did their job, bear got fresh tomatoes.

The second tale happened on our other property. The wife and I were wandering, just idly chatting, along the road that served as access to the back of our property. We were talking about how quiet animals, even bears, can move through the underbrush when they want to. I jokingly said one could be standing almost right beside us in the bush, and we would not know it. As I made this remark, I tossed a rock into the underbrush beside the road. Yep, you guessed it; it landed on or close to a bear. I said something memorable and suggested to the wife we move off at a faster pace. To my surprise, she was bending down picking up rocks. When I asked (in a very controlled voice hee hee) what the %^*@ she was doing, she said she wanted to see the bear. She was going to toss some more rocks at it so it would show itself. I explained to her that a rather upset bear weighing considerably more than both of us put together, was not something you wanted to @%^* off. So I moved her along, putting a safe distance between us and the bear.

This next little tale is a family affair, so to speak. This happened on the same property as the rock in the bush incident. I was just leaving for work in the morning, and a fine warm summer morning it was. As my hand started to open the outside door, I naturally looked out through the window in the door. You guessed it; a bear was looking back at me. Now I have seen bears before, but this one took me by surprise. At the time I owned a 1980 Mustang, which was parked under the carport. The bear, on all fours, was higher than my car. I walked back into the kitchen and told the wife. Now the two of us are standing looking at this bear, and we both had the same feeling: it was a grizzly bear. While I phoned the game warden, the wife and one son were up on the deck watching the bear. The bear moved to the back of the yard and made a few charges at the dogs in their run. My dogs, not being too bright, charged back. My wife or son, in defense of the dogs, tossed a patio chair at the bear. All I saw was it flying through the air. The next maneuver was to toss a pot at it; it mangled the pot. The bear moved off, and I phoned the neighbors to warn them. I had quite some difficulty convincing the game warden that it was a grizzly. After the neighbor watched it toss plywood around in his yard and called it in, they began to believe. They finally trapped the young two-year-old and shipped it out. I believe that story even made the local paper.

That's all I dare write about the bear encounters. I could tell you some tales of raccoons, but that can wait for now. I hope you all have a wonderful, bear able summer. See you again, I hope.

Hello from China

If anyone had told me a few years ago that I would be in China teaching English, I would have laughed. Well, I am not laughing and am in China teaching English. A couple of years ago, while I was an instructor for Saint John Ambulance, an acquaintance asked me why I was still in my hometown. I of course told them about the many, many things that make my hometown an ideal place to live and raise families. She smiled and said that was not what she meant. They knew me quite well and asked why, with my talents and abilities, I had not considered teaching overseas. One thing led to another, and soon I was a qualified TESL instructor headed for China.

The first thing that happened when I arrived in China was the person who was supposed to meet me at the Beijing airport was not there. Somehow, with no Chinese abilities, I found a hotel, booked a room, and used the Internet to track down my missing contact. Welcome to China. I was bundled onto an Air China jet and landed in the city of Gui Yang, province of Gui Zhou. This time I was met and taken by car to the No. 1 High School in the suburb of Jin Yang.

My bags were carried up to my apartment, the Chinese people left, and I had the weekend to myself. Oh, and they told me my classes started Monday. About this time, I was wondering what I had gotten into. The saving grace was that there are three other foreign teachers, one other Canadian and two Australians. They were my orientation for my first weekend in China.

It has now been almost nine weeks into my contract and things are settling in. I teach thirteen classes per week, with more than fifty students in each class. So far the language is coming to me slowly, and the cultural differences can be, well, different. Ask me sometime about Chinese bathrooms. The people are very friendly; the common worker or shopkeeper is honest and helpful. This does not mean you get the best price of course. Bargaining is part of the culture; you haggle over prices here; fun once you get the hang of it. One of the biggest things to get used to is the number of people, wall to wall. The population of the province I am in is equal to the total population of Canada. The city population of Gui Yang is almost equal to the population of British Columbia. Shoulder to shoulder is for real in the marketplaces here. I have been able to make one outing to n historic village built in the time of the Ming dynasty and hope to be able to do some sightseeing.

An Anniversary

The dictionary defines an anniversary as: "1. A day in the year on the date of which an event occurred in some preceding year." For us, this usually means birthdays, weddings, or the commencing of a business. But what do we do on these anniversaries? Yes, we celebrate the day, but we often reflect and sometimes plan for the next year or so. So, I reflected on my time experiences in China and my return home.

As with most things in life, the doing is different. You can research, read, and listen, but not until you experience it do you really begin to understand. (Do not apply this to all things in life.) As for living in a foreign culture, experiencing it is the only way to really learn. After the adrenaline rush and sensory overload subsided, my experiences became mostly normal. Living and working in China is, of course, very different than in Canada. But in some respects it is the same. I did my job every day, shopped for food, cooked, and, in short, existed. Then something wonderful happened, but not until I returned home. There is the culture shock of living in a foreign culture of course. Not understanding the language or customs makes for some interesting, and sometimes nerve-rattling experiences. But when you return to your own home, you get reverse culture shock, and it is quite different.

In China, it took almost the entire ten months to start to feel comfortable and function with some kind of ease. You begin to understand your frustrations, and start to live your life in their tempo, within their social guidelines. I found the Chinese people both wonderful and frustrating. (Sounds a lot like home, huh?) I would not even begin to call myself an expert, but I have some knowledge now. The cultural differences are there and in some ways frustrating. It is frustrating until you put aside your Western culture and go with theirs. This took me some time to do, but my frustration level went way down once I started to do this. I would never try to be Chinese: won't happen. But I did begin to live as a foreigner within their way of doing things. It's not as easy as it sounds sometimes. But we can work more on that this coming year. What about reverse culture shock?

Coming home was an eye-opener, almost as much as arriving in China. I was all excited and pumped up when I landed in Canada, happy to be back. Customs officials were nice and understood my excitement. It was when I got back home it hit. I was struck by the, "Oh you're back are you? Were you gone?" Hmmmmm. I found it as hard to fit back into life here as I had in China. Here I understood the language, but not the customs. As I sat in restaurants, I watched and listened to people; I noticed they were exactly where they were when I left. Hmmm. Now this is not a bad thing, but at first I did not understand it.

I had stood outside and was now able to look back in. In our day-to-day lives, we are so busy living it that we don't understand it. Each person has a life, not yours, theirs. This we know but often forget when it comes to family or close friends. I had just returned from a great adventure, but it had been *my* adventure. Everyone I met had been living their lives for ten months. They had their adventures, their highs and lows. To each of us, our lives are all we have. I had forgotten this. I wanted to overwhelm my family and friends with my stories, my adventure. What of theirs? They had stories to tell, adventures to relate. Ahh, I had to learn patience and humility. I found myself on the computer with friends in China, talking about things in China. In Canada, I talked (more than some people wanted me to) about my adventures in China, but it was different. In Canada, it was akin to showing them slides of my latest vacation. (Remember how that was, huh?) I got the hang of it just before I was off back to China, but I did learn a lot.

First, I tell people how I feel about them when I see them. It might be the last time; you never know. I don't apologize for my life, but I don't criticize others for theirs. I try to take things as they come and not get so excited (doctor's orders). I am not foolish with money, but if I lose it, I lose it, no big deal. I had slammed home to me again that the little things are what matter. A hug to the wife, or telling someone you love them. That is more important than the gifts you bring, because the real gift we give to each other is ourselves. I hope all of you who read these articles feel the good things I try to put in my words. I hope you all have more highs than lows in your lives, more smiles than tears. Take care.

Oh Those Embarrassing Moments

I have written several articles on what I would like to think of as the lighter side of life. I suppose some people could say they are those embarrassing moments we would all like to forget. Why? First of all, if anyone remembers any of those moments, they do so with love and a kinship of sorts. Yes, we have all had at least a couple of those things happen to us. On the other hand, if some people bring them up to embarrass you all over again, they should really get a life. Why do these things happen to otherwise perfectly sane and normal people? Why do we lock the keys in the car? Why do we say something completely, forgive me, stupid from time to time? Guess what? YOU'RE HUMAN, GET USED TO IT! But are those things really embarrassing? I mean, locking your keys in your car is an all too common thing; why be embarrassed? And saying something that is completely stupid really depends on the listeners, not you. Well, maybe anyway. We'll get back to that one. So, here is the first clue: who is embarrassed? Off we go, Dr. Ziggy's sense of self-1010. Relax, don't panic. I will not turn this into some kind of psych term paper; I did enough of those in university. We will keep this on the level where we all operate, real people, real language, and real world. First let's figure out embarrassing.

My dictionary states that embarrass means: "1. To make self-conscious and uncomfortable. 2. To involve in financial difficulties. 3. To hamper; impede. 4. To render difficult; complicate." Number 1 is all too familiar to us, right? Number 2 is not used too much to my knowledge; hell we are all financially embarrassed, and we have children, mortgages, and are constantly fighting inflation. Number 3 on the list I have never thought of, but if you do embarrass someone for your own gains, yes I suppose you could impede their personal development or career. Number 4 again hints at someone doing it to another person for their own self-importance or malicious enjoyment. Number 1 on the list is how we perceive an action we have done. That is, we feel embarrassed. But why? We feel uncomfortable or self-conscious because others make us feel that way. Definitions 3 and 4 indicate that to embarrass is to impede and make difficult. As embarrassment is a human feeling, it must mean to impede or make difficult a person's development by making them feel inadequate, self-conscious. Wow, do you think so? Think about it. Why did you feel embarrassed? You did not set out to do something that would make you feel self-conscious or uncomfortable did you? It is the audience, folks. The reaction of those that saw you do or say something that was perhaps a little humorous or, shall we say, not the norm. Now, why do some people laugh with you and others laugh at you? Hmmmmm.

As promised earlier, I will not go into psychological mind-twisting as I point out the various personality types and their interaction with society and personal relationships. Nahh. One of my best professors stated, "Psychology is the attempt to quantify common sense.

Unfortunately, in the real world, common sense is not that common."
In short, how do we define normal behavior? By exclusion, if you are
not a genius or a complete grapefruit mentally, you're normal. Check
out the bell curve we use in analytical research. You and I, folks,
are sitting in the 80 percent, give or take a few percentage points, of
all the psychological testing instruments out there. We are normal.
(Yes that last sentence was written that way on purpose.) Therefore,
of all those little things we do and say, at least 80 percent of them
are normal human behavior. We usually do something a little odd
because we are thinking of something else. I lock my keys in the car
when I am not thinking about where I am going or why. True, I am
at the moment preoccupied with other thoughts too much, ergo, slam
door with keys firmly in ignition. Oops. We do these little things
from time to time because we are not concentrating on what we are
doing, or sometimes saying. Why? One of my Chinese students had
the answer. They asked me what the English word was to describe,
for example, flying in the clouds like a bird. Ahh, daydreaming. The
student smiled and laughed; yes that was it. We daydream, or let
our mind wander sometimes when we are bored, or when we are not
interested in something, or we are just totally confused. (That was
the case for me in most of my classes during my school life.) I was
the world's most prolific daydreamer, well in with the 80 percent of
my class anyway, maybe more. The other big one for us as adults is
stress of course. We often worry and fret over paying bills, etc., etc.,
etc. Why?

First, daydreaming is a very healthy thing to do. Most great
artists and scientists are great daydreamers. How else could they get
out of the box and come up with their unique ideas? Of course the
problem is timing. Don't daydream while driving, working, or in your

classes. That can lead not only to embarrassment, but also to serious injury. So do your daydreaming at an appropriate time, like on the deck or soaking up rays at the beach with a cold one. Well, whatever you like to do. My best ideas (or not) come when I am just watching the life around me, taking time to smell the roses, so to speak. My wife tells me it is because of my great memory; I believe morbid was a word she used, oh well. So daydreaming is a normal and healthy thing to do, just do it at an appropriate time. What about stress?

Folks, believe it or not, we need stress to survive; the problem is when we get overloaded. Someone wrote, "Give me the intelligence to see the problems around me, and the wisdom to recognize those I can do something about and those I cannot." Something like that; my apologies to the author of that statement. In short, we can't fix the problems of the world, no matter how much we want to. All we can do is try to fix our little part of it. In your personal life, well, as they sometimes say, "shit happens." Recognize it, forget it, and move on. I used to make lists of things to do when I ran my business, also for my personal life. It really helped me realize that some things were just not in the cards for me to do anything about, so, delegate it. Also, when looking at a problem of some kind, don't look at the whole problem; cut it down to size and deal with it piece at a time. The best medicine for stress is laughter—and exercise according to my doctor (damn cholesterol levels anyways). So, what have I just said to you, hmmmm? Well, let's see if we can put it all together.

We are embarrassed because of something we say or do. We often do or say these things because we are not concentrating on the task at hand. This can be caused by boredom, confusion, or lack of interest. (Note to male readers, don't be doing this near your wife. The consequences could make an atomic bomb look like a firecracker.) We are also sometimes not paying attention due to our preoccupation with some kind of problem in our lives, stressed out as they say. When we do or say this supposedly embarrassing thing, it means nothing except if we have the audience. If no one sees it, no embarrassment. So all the things I write about are just normal human behavior, not meant as any great philosophical outlook on life. I just took the time to remember, with love, events in my humdrum existence. It has nothing to do with embarrassment or embarrassing moments, and everything to do with love and good memories from a good life. If you don't have them, you have nothing to offset what psychologists call critical life events. We all know the downsides to our mortal existence and the battle with inflation, etc. Those are things we can do nothing about, so I smile do my best and carry on. I hope my little articles help you smile and perhaps bring back your own good memories. Take care of yourselves and keep smiling. It makes people wonder what you have been up to.

It's a Buddy's World

A More Philosophical Outlook

Welcome to part 2 of my little collection of articles. In this section I focus less on the family things and more on some things my readers talked about. That is, things that are part of our combined human existence. I try to maintain my positive outlook, but do not treat the more serious with any kind of disrespect or glibness. I hope you, the reader, enjoy your journey into my world.

If

Well I don't understand it, so maybe some of you can help me. The word "if"—such a small word, only two letters, but it can mess up our little minds. What if, if only, if I had the chance, if I could have, and on and on. My wife and I were talking one evening; that's what older people do when the kids are grown up and left home. We were doing that reminiscing thing; you know, remembering when the kids did this and that. Then we started to remember how we had met, our friends, and old flames. We wondered where we might be if … . It is hard to say, of course, too many things are unknown. But it can be interesting. My wife surprised me by saying she would have liked to have been an airline flight attendant. Well, she was built like the proverbial cement outhouse, with great legs, and was bilingual. She could have done it and probably would have if … . Well, you know the rest. What about me? Don't really have a clue. I did join the military, which was one of my dreams, so to speak, so I probably would have remained and retired at forty-five, kind of boring but safe. But what-if?

What if I had married one of my other girlfriends, or she had married one of her other boyfriends. What would our lives have been like? Would we have the same number of children, live where we live, would we even still be alive? Now there's a scary and depressing idea. I tried to imagine what my life would have, or could have, been like with some of my other girlfriends as a wife. Hmmmm. Well, first of all, they are old girlfriends for a reason; we broke up. That is a bad sign for a harmonious relationship, right? OK, OK, I'll try. Well, after thinking about it, the pictures were blurry and not that good. Perhaps it would have worked out with them, perhaps this and that would have happened, but it didn't. I had the luxury of seeing some of my old girlfriends in later years; yep, we broke up for good reasons. Whew, it could have been me instead of, oh well never mind. Seriously, many of our old flames have grown into fine men and women, but the whatever it is, magic or connection, is not there because it really never was. So, what if is merely a mind game for older people whose children have grown up and left home. Maybe?

I actually don't think if is an option in our lives. We are who we are and where we are because of choices and decisions we have made along the way. Sometimes we made those choices without thinking, or they were made for us by the other people involved in our lives at that time. The situation we were in, and other variables, (my psych professors will like that one), simply gave us no choice. They say that by age five, a person's personality is set. Man, I guess that's why I mess up so much; I am just a five-year-old running wild. Anyway, we tend to react to people, places, and things in a set way. We like who, what, and where because of some inner force in our being. Some call it personality, and others put different names on it. I am not sure what it is, but I have this thing called a sixth sense; it has warned me of danger and sometimes of paths to take in my life. Oh, I have heard it called vibes, a feeling, a gut feeling, instinct, and a few other things as well. So this sixth sense combined with my five-year-old personality—oops, my personality—to become my guiding whatever you wish to call it. We tend to what-if something to death when we just don't listen to ourselves. Ya, I could what-if it as well, but what for? You make decisions and choices, and sometimes you feel like you blew it. Guess what? You didn't. You were intended to blow it; that was the plan. Whose plan? Nope, I am not going there this time. OK, OK, I'll stretch out my neck again, what the hell.

I am not a Bible thumper folks, and neither devil nor saint, but I do believe there is something in each of us. What it is, well there are many theologians and philosophers who have made careers out of that one. All I know is I was supposed to die once, and did not. I fell off a cliff at about age six or eight and was given twenty-four hours to live. The doctors told my poor parents there was nothing they could do; my brain was hemorrhaging, and my skull plate was partially crushed and shifted. I obviously did not die, and I can remember it all to this day as if it just happened. I still see the face of my friend looking down as I fell away, the car that almost ran us over as they carried me to my home. I remember passing out in my mom's kitchen, the taxi ride, my sister yelling for him to drive faster. I remember what some people call a near-death experience—no, not a bright white light, people, a golden one. A sense of peace, calm, warmth and contentment surrounded me; at the time, that seemed to be just before I woke up. Then I was awake and back to normal, well normal for me that is. God, heaven, angels? I don't know. But many times I have seen others have similar experiences. They walk away from horrible accidents without a scratch, while others die from a simple slip in their own living room. There is the story of one of my friends who lay on the bottom of a lake for almost half an hour before they could get to him. He is alive and well with a family today. Why? I believe we are all here to fulfill some kind of purpose, to be part of certain people's lives in various ways, at certain times.

There is a friend of mine who believes we go through certain experiences to learn a lesson, things such as humility, compassion, and empathy. Perhaps my friend is correct. I really don't have a clear answer. If I did—oops, there's that if word again—I would share it with you all. Perhaps we what-if things when we are trying to find our inner companion, that peace of mind, feeling of contentment, calmness, and being at peace with ourselves and the world around us. I do know that when you what-if things about your life in a calm and reflective manner, you find that inner companion. So go ahead and what-if to your heart's content, just do it with a sense of reflection, not as an accusation that you messed up somehow. You didn't. You are where you are for some kind of reason. They tell me when you discover the reason or reasons you get this thing called wisdom. Hmm, wonder what that's like? With this wisdom, we are supposed to become one with our inner companion and have all the warmth, peacefulness, contentment, and peace of mind we are all looking for. Well, if I am as good a writer as I think I am, I just gave that to you. Man, the ego of some people. Take care people, smile and carry on with your part in the grand scheme of things. Someday I truly hope we all have peace of mind, contentment of spirit, warmth of love, and the calmness in the knowledge of we are where we are needed to be. Take care of yourselves.

Fear, or the Lack of It

"Don't look at it as being afraid, look at it as the same feeling you have Christmas morning. Not fear, but excited anticipation." That little statement was said to me by the head instructor during a professional driver's training course. I had been trying so hard to learn all about driving 18-wheelers that I was becoming what I interpreted as afraid, or nervous. The head instructor, who was a veteran at training drivers, saw what I was going through and offered his advice" Being scared or nervous is just like being excited, they are the same feeling to the body. So, you are excited with anticipation, not afraid of making mistakes". Sounds easy enough, but of course it does take some discipline and conscious effort. The statement has stayed with me over the years, and I wondered if it would fit all or most situations. What is fear anyway?

The dictionary tells us fear is an agitated feeling aroused by awareness of actual or threatening danger, trouble, etc. It goes on to say things such as the anticipation of dreaded or unwanted events. Sounds bloody ominous to me, I must admit. In the realm of the study of human behavior, it is often called the fight-or-flight response. The dictionary definition of excitement or excited uses terms like agitated, aroused, or stirred up. To stimulate strong emotions or arouse strong feelings were also terms used to describe the feeling of excitement. My driving instructor has a point then; it is the anticipated end result that not only evokes the emotions, but tells our mind to be afraid or excited. What about the lack of fear? Trying to be logical here, our society uses words like courage, fearlessness, and confidence to mean the opposite of fear. Well, here is where I have a problem.

Courage is not the opposite of fear. It is the reaction you have even though you are afraid, sometimes very afraid. I cannot remember who made this statement, but it goes like this: "A hero is a frightened person who runs the wrong way." So again, it is a reaction, and so far holds to my concepts of fear or lack of it. Confidence comes from knowledge of a situation and an understanding of what is happening, not the overcoming of fear. Now for some situations, such as public speaking, there could be room for argument against my simplistic approach. But I still feel that even in the realm of public speaking, you do it by being trained, prepared, and still afraid. The difference is you do not allow the fear to force you to react by running away, so to speak. Again, it is the reaction, or the mind-set if you like. Fear is real, not imagined. Even if you perceive the reason for the fear to be imaginary, you will react in the same manner. It is not lack of fear, it is as my instructor stated: "Understanding the reactions your body is having, and modifying the reason for those reactions, is the key". Does it always work?

I have known fear, as have most of us. I have reacted to events with the inability to move physically, these can be symptoms of such conditions as posttraumatic stress syndrome, panic attacks, or a catatonic state as a result of severe psychological trauma. I overcame my fears as they came—sometimes quickly—by reacting to the event or circumstance. I often ran the wrong way. Other times I had to analyze and develop a strategy to work with the fear I felt or my reaction to some unknown fear. Medications to rebalance neurotransmitters or to reduce anxiety are methods to begin to get hold of the situation. But, it is not until you realize fear is always there and is an ally you can work with that you can overcome fear. It is the words and meanings we often put to them that sometimes work against us.

Courage, fearlessness, and confidence are not the opposite of fear or being afraid. They are you working with fear as part of you, your ally. There is no such thing as lack of fear. Fear is as much a part of our lives as breathing. It is in dealing with our own particular reactions to our fears that we move forward. If people wish to call it courage, fearlessness, confidence, or some other thing, fine. But it is not lack of fear; there is no such thing.

Good Old Negativism

Have you ever noticed how some people just love to rain on your parade? You know the type. You come bouncing into a room high on a great feeling about something in your world, which you just have to share with your friends or associates. After you do, you don't get the expected upbeat, positive response. In fact, you feel like someone just let all the air out of your happy balloon. Why? Why is it that some people just can't stand to see someone else happy or optimistic? Is it jealousy or envy? Do they think you are wrong to share your good feelings with others?

Some people say it is to steal your power; a controlling personality will do this. I suppose that is one possibility. I have read that people often do this because of some deep-rooted social or psychological problem they may not even be aware of. Wow, heavy stuff. Could it be that some people are so anal they can't imagine the world outside of themselves? What do you think, Sigmund? (That's Freud, the father of psychoanalytical thought, boys and girls.) Indeed, some of the deeper thinkers may be right about the reasons for negativity, but

I have a different spin, surprise, surprise. Let's see if we can figure this out together, shall we?

First, think of someone in your circle who is the rain cloud over your parade, that person who just has to pop your happiness balloon. I'll give you a few minutes (hmm, hmmm, la de da hmm). OK, got them! Now, try to remember a time when they were negative about something you were happy about, and they just stomped it to death, so to speak. Got it! Good! Next, try to remember the situation you were in when you told your personal black cloud your happy news. OK, now if you can, try to remember the words you used and the words of their response. How are we doing? Haven't lost you yet I hope. Be careful now, don't try to be all analytical; just gather the information. OK, if you have it together, you might be feeling a little bit like you did when this event actually happened. Stop that, I told you not to analyze, just remember. OK, here we go.

Go back and reread the article to this point, paying attention to how you feel as you read the words. I'll wait right here for you. Go on read them before you move on to the next part, no cheating.

Now if you are here reading this part, and did as I asked, you should have your answer right. No? OK, OK. After reading the first part, did you think this was going to be a serious, maybe depressing thing to read? After reading the next part, did your feelings about what you were reading change? It is like that old saying my grandmother used to use, "It's not what you say, it's how you say it that matters." This does not just apply to the spoken word, but to the words or thoughts that bounce around in our little noggins (brain for you under-fifty crowd). It is not anyone's words that are negative; it is how we perceive the intent of these words, and their effect on our emotions. Their words can be negative, but we don't have to receive them and keep bouncing them around in out little brain box do we? To hell with them, folks! If you're happy, damn it, be happy! That's it. No great philosophical edict, no heavy psychological analysis, not in the slightest, my friends. Place your hands firmly on your hips, project your tongue past your front teeth, and hang onto your brightly colored happiness balloon. Oh, before you move on, put your tongue back in.

Law and Disorder?

I recently returned to Canada for my vacation. While up on news here at home, I was saddened to see a number of violent deaths among the police. As a young child, I had idolized the RCMP and was proud of the Canadian history they represented. When I grew into adulthood, my idolization turned to respect, and my pride of the Canadiana they represent, intensified.

I am old enough to recall seeing the RCMP wearing their Smokey the Bear hats on duty. In old movies you might see the same hat on U.S. Forest Rangers; I believe some U.S. police forces still wear them. I was three or four years old when I met my first police officer. He had come to our yard to answer a complaint against one of my older brothers. I looked to see very large and high brown riding boots. Looking upward, I saw this very tall man in a brown tunic, wearing the Smokey the Bear hat and dark blue pants with a yellow stripe down the legs. He smiled and asked something, to which I nodded my head and ran for my mother. As a young child, this image made me feel safe; this policeman was a giant to a three- or four-year-old.

No bad guy would dare go up against him. Of course I still grew into a typical pre-teen and teenager. The early image of the police had blurred a little.

During my teenage years I purchased a motorcycle. I liked to ride my bike fast and yes, show off. On one occasion, I was forced into oncoming traffic by a good citizen who hated bike riders, and to avoid death, I jumped my bike up onto the sidewalk. Unfortunately I was now very angry, cat walked my bike, and rode approximately one block on the sidewalk. Yep, guess who saw that? Being a typically observant person, I did not see the police cruiser with its accompanying policeman. I roared back onto the road and sailed down the street, stopping at a red light several blocks later. A horn drew my attention; behind me was the police car, lights flashing and policeman smiling. Uh oh. Once pulled over, I explained to the policeman what had happened; he had not seen it but believed me. He let me off with a warning. Wow, they are human. Unfortunately this good-hearted policeman did not make the desired impression on me.

Over the next few weeks, I continued my reckless behavior with both motorcycle and car. I never did the doughnut thing with the car, but could lay you a strip of rubber any drag racer would be proud of. My speeds were always above the posted limit, except in school zones and parks. One night some friends and I were cruising around town, as we used to call it, when we came upon an "opportunity." I came around a corner too fast, and somebody was waving a sign. (I noticed that as I passed him.) Well, we hit the largest puddle of water I have ever seen, sending a wall of water in three directions as we careened through it. As we continued speeding down the highway, we talked excitedly about what had just happened and got a stupid idea: let's do it again. So we circled around and struck again, soaking the highway workers. Hell, that was so much fun, we just had to do it again. On our fourth or fifth run at it, we noticed something new. A man was standing in the road waving a flashlight. Oh well. As we smashed through the water, sending a tidal wave in three directions, we saw who the flashlight holder was: RCMP. "Oh shit," I believe was the phrase used in unison in the car. I am pretty sure we made that policeman not only very wet, but also very, very mad that night. I roared off, and we were soon sitting in one of our hiding spots. Three hours later, we ventured back out onto the road.

A few nights later, we were driving around the sleepy town, ending up at a local schoolyard. One of my friends had a basketball, and we were going to play some moonlight hoops. Ahhh, but we were teenagers, and this could not be just a night basketball game. (Man, I wish we could sometimes just stop being too smart for our own good.) Of course not; we were going to play car basketball. So we began to run up and down the outdoor basketball court, shooting baskets from the car. (Only the driver could not shoot; after all, we had to have a couple rules.) Ya, that funny car with the lights on top showed up, and we were off and running again. (Maybe it was our not stopping and getting away that was making these guys mad.) We ditched the police and, feeling very smug, carried on with our evening of idiocy. It was around 2 a.m., and I, alone now, was heading home. I was roaring up a hill when a set of headlights popped up behind me. *Hee, hee, the cops*, I said smugly to myself. I drove the speed limit from that point until he pulled me over. This policeman was not a happy camper. I wondered if he was the water baby, but never did find that out. Anyway, he ranted and raved, looked over my license and insurance, then said he was going to phone my parents.

In my day, it was not the police you worried about, it was Dad and Mom. They could and would make your life miserable and painful. My father was on the phone with the police when I walked into the house. Folks, you should have seen me. I did the greatest "I am an innocent kid and they are picking on me" routine. (Little @#%^&**, right?) So this fast-talking, look you in the face, I am innocent, little you know what dodged the bullet. Unfortunately, I had angered the wrong people: the guys in uniform who carry guns and enforce the law. So it was not a brilliant strategy to continue, right? I was intelligent, folks, even as a kid, but not always smart.

My bad behavior continued in one form or another, and then a few things happened. First, I did notice I had become the object of attention; more police cars were in my neighborhood and behind my car now. One day I had a vehicle run a red light on me. I ditched my bike to avoid being killed, and slid into a fence. A police car sat and watched the whole thing, but did not make a move. I went to the police station and ranted and raved. I was told it was my fault; I was driving with undo care and attention. This just made me cockier and more rebellious. (I think that was their plan.) I began to get tickets for everything and anything. It was inside the law of course, and to the letter of the law. At a stop sign, if my wheels never came to a compete stop, ticket for Bonzo. The law states a complete stop, which means wheels are not turning AT ALL. This went on for months. I even had them parking outside my yard, waiting for me to head out. No, people, this was not harassment; they can park wherever they want. They also give out tickets to idiots, part of the job. Well it happened; I finally got enough tickets and points to win the prize: a suspended license. When I surrendered my license, the police were very nice and did try to explain. I could take a driver's training course and get my license reinstated. I did not at that time. No, I ranted and stormed out. (Hey I was a teenager, testosterone, hormones, etc.) Is there a moral to this story? I don't know, but I will tell you what I learned.

Over the next several years, I had interactions with RCMP and other police forces, but not as adversaries. Years later I did take that driver training and became a professional driver. As I wander through this life, listening to and watching people, I hear and see many things that are negative in their intent toward the RCMP and police in general. Well, perhaps some of it is true; there are bad cops. There are even dirty cops, but they are not all like that. They are people, human beings, and they do a job that is dangerous, stressful, and for the most part thankless. Those policemen in my youth were actually trying to save my butt. I was either going to kill myself or someone else, and believe me, folks, it almost happened a few times. Without harassing me or bullying me, they were trying to keep me alive and off a certain path in life. They cared! So thank you to all who have taken up the profession of RCMP officer. You may not be the most welcome sight to some people, but you are to a lot of us. We remember the courage, the history, and the service you have given to this country, including going overseas and into war zones. Don't be like some of us, disillusioned with the law and its apparent inability to keep citizens safe. Believe in what you do. Most of us in this country do.

Reflection

Well it has happened. One week ago I celebrated yet another birthday; this one gets me closer to my sixth decade. The people where I work took me out for a birthday meal, complete with a very large cake. It was nice of them to do this, but I found myself not wanting to be there. I chastised myself heavily for this; they were being kind and I was being what, bored? Hmmm. The nonparty mood stayed with me, and I even found it an effort to carry on a conversation. Being the type of person I am, I tried to analyze why I was reacting in this manner. This self-analysis moved on toward a much deeper look at where I am and how I got here at the age of fifty-five.

This journey through my past brought me a sense of peace with the odd pang of embarrassment. You remember the times when you zigged, wondering what would life be like now if you had zagged instead. The many paths you chose in this journey called life—why did you choose them and what would have happened if you had chosen another? The many times you said something and regretted saying it almost as soon as the words left your mouth. There were the times you were silent, when words might have been needed but you could not find them. Some action or reaction you did, then wondered why you had done this without giving yourself time to perhaps have done it another way. There were the times when you did nothing and, you think now, something should have been done. The person I am now, how am I different from the one who was once young and full of defiance? Hmmmm, well the defiance part is still there. I have been called a rebel looking for a cause by some of my friends. The boat rocker, the wave slapper, the one who always asks, Why? Oh well, it does make for a lot of colorful memories. Looks like I am where I am, who I am, and for that matter what I am because of me, well mostly anyway. You always affect others on this journey, and they affect you as well. Your choice of friends, social activities, even your spouse all affects you, of course. So did I find my answer ? Oh ya!

Oh ... I suppose you want me to tell you, right? I enjoy many things in life, but watching and listening to people are two that I have done every day, all my life. The amazing thing is that I can remember it all: the faces, the events, the conversations. Ya, that's right for those that still owe me money. At first, this strange ability caused me pain; some things you wish you could forget. As I got older, these memories gave me information and peace. I realized that, even though I like to think I am a person who is intelligent, even perceptive, I rely more on my sixth sense. I listen to that inner voice that tells you, "No, don't go in there," or, "Yes, yes, do it, do it!" I have listened to the inner child in me all my life. The part of us that is innocent, curious, adventurous, and does not know the phrase, "It can't be done," or, "Act your age." The phrase my inner child hates is, "When are you going to grow up!" I always ask it, "What to you is grown up?" I of course get all the stock answers about responsibility, stability, growth (this one usually means money and or power), and being politically adept in your social skills. Hmmmm, sounds boring as hell to me, no thanks. Folks, don't listen to me; you have your own inner voice, listen to that. Some people call it your heart, listening to your soul, I don't know. There is that part of us that is alive with a sense of curiosity, adventure. It sees the bad things in this life, but helps us move past them. It helps us to make the next person feel good with a simple smile and simple pleasant greeting. It tells you to play in the sandbox sometimes with the toys, to laugh, but most important, be fluid. We are moving on this journey all the time; be free and go with it and let others do the same. I smile with great respect and happiness for those who have worked at the same job until they retired. Great for you. It is not me. I found me, and I like me. Those who like me too are welcome to drift along beside me for the journey. Those who think I am a complete irresponsible nutcase, not a problem. I will give you a smile from my heart, wish you all the best in your life, and drift onward down the river of life. I try to spread more good feelings than bad ones during my journey, give more to others than I take (no, folks, that does not mean material things). I give *me* to them: friendship, love, compassion and understanding. The pay isn't great, but maybe the retirement package is. After all, our journey will end. Well, that is another aspect of my inner child that an editor might let me tell you about sometime. Happy birthday to me.

Wherein Lies Truth

"The truth and nothing but the truth": a line used in courtroom dramas. When we are young, we are often told by our elders to always tell the truth. So what happens? When you become older and wiser, maybe your date asks you if she looks OK. So what will you answer? Will you tell her you do not like her dress, her hair, her perfume? Not a chance; you lie. We say something tongue in cheek, we do not mean what we say, and we lie. We lie to avoid punishment, embarrassment, responsibility, rejection. But why? We did not start out as liars; we were told to tell the truth.

I have heard statements such as, "Being honest gets you nothing." The person was referring perhaps to material gains, promotion, or career advancement. What do I get for telling the truth? Well, I do not have to tell more lies to substantiate the first one. I do not have to remember what I said to whom, so I don't get my stories mixed up. It is easier on me that way. So far sounds good. But the problem is the initial lie. Why would we tell that one? Is it just that we are caught in a weak moment, a temporary hesitation of our thought processes?

OK, I can live with that; I will just have to tell the truth eventually with an explanation. This can be a little embarrassing perhaps, but it is a livable option. What about the calculating premeditation of fabrication?

This person sets out to deceive, to lie, for either personal gain or satisfaction. Is this the person we do not like, the one we think of when we think of liars. The con artist, the rip-off artists, the frauds: these are the liars we do not like. These individuals systematically defraud other people with lies to gain, in some cases, both material and emotional gratification. We forgive the occasional white lie, the tongue-in-cheek statements, usually because the individual will tell the truth when pressed or at a better time, and explain why they told the lie. But the con artist, the rip-off artist, and the fraud will admit to their lying when caught as well. Some of us even come to admire these people; we admire their ingenuity, as we call it. Maybe it is the motives behind the lies that make the difference. If I lie to a woman and say, "Yes, your dress looks fine," maybe she wanted the truth. Maybe she does not like the dress and wanted another opinion to confirm this. No, a lie is a lie, no matter how you slice it. As we grew up, we learned about diplomacy and tact. That is, how to tell the truth without being blunt, or how to tell someone only what they need to know. Rather than saying the dress looks like a sack of flour on your lady friend, you could say, "It looks fine, but I am not sure it is right for you. There seems to be something odd about it." Wherein lies the truth, the truth, the whole truth, and nothing but the truth? Is it what we sometimes serve up with diplomacy and tact? A lie is a lie, and truth is truth. Is this a problem?

Even in our society today, we are told to tell the truth. Remember the courtroom thing? But why in the courtroom? Is it the truth they want, or does someone want to win something? The truth is based on physical evidence in a court of law, not on verbal communication. So what I say on the stand can only substantiate or confuse the presented physical evidence. It is not truth they want from you in a verbal sense; they want collaboration of the physical evidence presented. No, it is not the courtroom that wants truth; they deliver up the law through the process of an established legal system. Wherein lies the truth?

Truth lies in only the most innocent of people: the very young or those who have somehow come to terms with themselves. The baby you hold in your arms is total trust and truth. As we grow things happen, situations, events, and we either remain true or waver off course. We should tell the truth all the time. It saves a lot of pain down the road for us and those whose lives we affect. The truth lies within each of us. The problem is having the courage to tell the truth and accept the consequences. It is not the truth that is the problem, it is our lack of courage to stand and accept the consequences of the truth. A lie is a lie. Truth is truth. Which one we choose to use at any given time is up to us. Life is really nothing more complicated than choices. We just sometimes lack the courage to accept the responsibility for our actions or words, and to accept the consequences that either may have. The truth lies within each of us. Use it always.

It Was Nothing

There was no loud thunder, no lightning, and no wind. Nothing warned you of the oblivion, of the darkness, of the end. It was just there in your face. You feel like a trapped animal, all resources gone, all escapes futile, nowhere to run, nowhere to hide. It is over.

Have you ever had this feeling? Have you ever been held in place emotionally, physically, mentally? Frozen, unmovable, empty, all has been poured out of you. Where does it come from, why and how? I don't know. I just know it hurts, it scares you, and it shakes your very being. You wonder how you got to this place; you remember laughter, being full of pride and unstoppable, not anymore. Who did it? Why did they do it? How did they do it? Did you let them? Did they do it with or without your help? You claw at possibilities, at straws. As one after the other break or prove illusionary, you feel panic.

You can't sleep, you can't work, and you can't have fun. You lash out, you run, and you hide. Your eyes dart around, looking for something, an ally, a friend, a warm hand. You stand helplessly as all you hoped and wished for stands there, out of your reach. You are stung by the laughter, the looks, and the silence of others. Patience has gone, time has run out. Your mind races, searching for solutions to problems you no longer comprehend. Thoughts become jumbled, emotions unchained. Madness seems to possess you; you feel it ripping at your sanity. Then an eerie calmness comes stealing into your consciousness. You smile and nod your head. With a tear in your eye, your throat choked with emotion, and a calm heart, you end it.

There is no warm glowing sunshine, no sweet-smelling carpet of flowers, and no gentle breeze. Nothing warned you of the epiphany, the light, or the calmness. You feel like you are outside your body, no worries, no panic, and no desperation. It is over.

Have you ever had this feeling? Have you ever just drifted emotionally, physically, mentally in slow, measured purposeful steps but with no goal or direction, neither leading nor following? You feel strange, outside yourself, outside of all around you. Where does this come from, why and how? I don't know. I just know it calms, it pacifies me, and it soothes my very being. You wonder how you got to this place; you remember anger, being full of rage, frozen with panic, but not anymore. Who did it? Why did they do it? Did you let them? Did they do it with or without your help? You pass through your environment, your part of space and time. As each object comes to your sight, you feel nothing but calmness and peace.

Your eyes feel heavy, you feel a sense of purpose, and you smile inside and out. You feel gentleness; you stroll slowly into the open. Your eyes calmly scan your surroundings, searching for nothing, merely enjoying what you see. You move slowly, ambling onward in any direction you choose, seeing for the first time that which is your hopes and dreams. You are calmed by the silence, by the absence of noise, of others near you. The anger has gone, time has run out. Your mind is clearly in focus with your spirit, there are no problems to be solved. You see only objects to observe. You stroll up to them and experience the moments. Sanity has not been ripped from you by some madness; the madness has been moved away by the sanity. There is a strange feeling of enlightenment that glows throughout your consciousnesses. You smile the crooked smile with a gentle snort, and nod your head. With dry eyes and a calmness of emotion, you gaze upon the end. With one more crooked smile, gentle snort, and nodding of the head, you end it. It was the beginning.

What Round Are We In? (Round 2?)

Well, for those of you who have read my other articles, this is me back in China. The publisher asked me to write something, and I thought, *Piece of cake*. Hmmmmm. Well, so far, no cake. I went through some tough times both during my vacation in Canada and now back here in China. I wrote a great letter, but you folks will never see it; it was private. So I know I can still write, but what do I write for you, the audience of my published articles? My offhanded sense of humor seems to attract readers; my humorous look at normal life seems to be well received. I do have a good sense of humor, all my friends and family will agree, but what if it can't be used? As all of you know, not everything in this life is funny, especially when it is happening or just after it happened. Some things in this life seem to tear up our emotions, sending them into downward spirals that seem to be endless. Depression, anger, and fear are all very real emotions to us. Those of us who try to be upbeat and humorous most of the time fall into a trap. When we get depressed, angry, or become afraid, our humor is often used as a defense. But it is tainted humor. Our normal happy-go-lucky outlook is not laced with love and compassion. No, now the humor is slightly bitter, sometimes even sarcastic and biting. No, folks, I am not depressed, angry, or afraid. But I would like to give you a perspective from the side of the happy-go-lucky fellow.

Sometimes it is hard to maintain the positive outlook on life; you have all been there I know. So what do I do? Well, I write. Writing for me is both therapeutic and fun. My feelings can pour out of me in the written word without the emotional variables of body language and facial expressions. Cold? No, not really. I feel good writing can evoke emotions in the reader and actually touch them deeply. If my writing does not do it, then I go out to the woodshed and see how much wood I can split. Writing is easier on my body, but splitting wood is good for it as well. So I find both a physical and intellectual outlet. For an emotional outlet, I end up talking to a very close friend or my wife. With the initial internal turmoil taken care of, now I can talk and listen with a nonjudgmental mind. Well, at least I have a better chance. I am a very emotional person, so most conversations with me can get lively. Depression for me is the easiest to take care of.

I have been so depressed I have said and done things that were way out of character for me. The important thing is I recognized it. I try to figure out why I am depressed, usually by writing down my feelings and any person, thing, or place that may be involved. As I write, the fog begins to clear and I find the source or sources. Next, put it in perspective. If it is anything I can do something about, I do it. If it is something that is beyond my control, I recognize the fact and move along with my life. Talking things out with a confidant is also very important. The process has no timeline, and it is not always easy, but it works. Often those outside a problem have great clarity;

being involved, you can't see the forest for the trees. The danger for us happy-go-lucky people here is others. They don't seem to know how to handle the "always in a good mood" person who is depressed, upset, or morose. "You will get over it," is one of their favorites. Those of us with a positive outlook on life need a life preserver once in a while as well. What about anger?

Anger is as common to most of us as love; it has been called the two sides of the same coin. Oh yes, I get angry. In fact, sometimes I become downright incensed with rage. Is this good or bad? The emotion is neither; it is how you handle it that makes it good or bad. Anger can be a very positive thing, believe it or not. I get absolutely incensed about some social issues. The stupidity of some governments can send me into an almost maniacal state of helplessness. (Wow, good words huh?) I believe we should allow ourselves to be angry, but to act positively with that anger. My mind can become focused and sharp when I am angry. I use what skills and gifts I have to address the source of the outrage. If it is a social issue, I write about it, talk about it, or get involved with groups trying to do something positive. Stupidity in governments, hmmm. Well, I write to MPs, or if I really want action, I write an article for a paper or magazine. Politicians are politicians; bad publicity is like the Black Death to them. So voice your displeasure and send the message to where it will do the most good. If the anger is from one individual, use the "Can I do anything about it" rule. Talk to them; let them know how you feel and why. They are not obligated to understand or respond in a positive manner, but doing it releases your anger in a positive way. No matter the outcome, you did your bit; if they don't, too bad, you move along. The problem for us happy-go-lucky people is it is such a shock to some people. What, the party clown is upset? Ya, it happens.

Remember, folks, we are all human. Even the always-smiling positive people have bad days, weeks, and sometimes months. So you get your chance to be a friend in need. We all can use those from time to time. What about fear?

Fear is with us all the time. I used to wake up at night, unable to sleep because of fear or worry. My children: can I protect them from all the bad things in this world? My wife: can I protect her from all that could go wrong? Fear of poverty: can I support my family? Things happen in a person's job or career that can bother them. After an injury, and I have had a few, I have known fear. I was injured in an industrial accident and unable to move. Being paralyzed was my greatest fear. It took several months, actually a little over a year, to recover fully, but I did. Part of it was I just would not give up; I would not give into my fear and accept it. I fought it. Even if I had lost, I would have known I tried my best to overcome it. So, first you have to define if it is fear you are feeling? Worry is a kind of fear, but it is one that you can handle. Again, if you can do something about it, do it, if not, accept it. Fear can, in some cases, be protection. I have a fear of heights. Well, falling from a high place can hurt you, so I don't see a problem with the fear. I just know I will never be a roofer, mountain climber, or chimney sweep. All joking aside, I know that in some cases, fear, depression, or anger can interfere with a person's life. If that is the case, then you should seek professional help. As with all things, talk to a friend or a confidant. Understanding from others is what is sought, especially by us jokesters. People seem to depend on us for the feel better boost, but sometimes we are unable to give it. From time to time, everyone needs someone who is understanding, compassionate, and caring. Even just a good nonjudgmental listener is sometimes a godsend.

Wow, that was a different article wasn't it. Well, it comes from the heart, folks, it really does. I had writer's block and could not get through it. I ran possible subjects through my mind, even wrote several pages, then trashed them. While attempting to write about something, I realized I was avoiding my own feelings. So, I wrote them down, and then edited them for public display, so to speak. Working in a foreign country far from your culture, family, and friends keeps you in an almost-constant state of emotional readiness. Between adapting to the life and trying to carry out your job, you are running on reserve batteries a lot. This article is for you to enjoy. I hope you do, but it was one for me. I needed to bare my soul a bit. Life is a journey as I and others have said. On that journey, you come to many crossroads; you have decisions to make, sometimes big ones. You get depressed, angry, and afraid, usually because you have not yet chosen the path. That is the problem. The other problem can be you have chosen the path, but now are second-guessing your decision. Hindsight is 20/20. Yep, maybe you should or should not have done something in your past, but hey, that's the past and it is gone. Let it go. My ship is under sail once more, and the captain is back at the helm. He may be unsure, scared, but he is in control of what he can control. I thank all of you who have read what I have written. It means a great deal to me. I shall keep it up, and I hope you will continue to get amusement, joy, maybe a smile, out of it. Take care of yourselves, people, and remember to allow yourself to love and be loved.

The Two of Me
Can I Be Put Back Together Again?

I want to take you on a trip. This journey will have to be with your mind, and you will have to use your imagination; sorry, I am poor and cheap. The journey we are going on is revealing and perhaps a little frightening, so take your time and find a nice place to read this article. Recently, someone very close to me had a traumatic emotional incident; I was there and witnessed it. I feel this article is important to you, as it has to do with stress and how we usually do not handle it. It has to do with signs and symptoms that my friend ignored, until it was too late; my friend literally fell apart like a mirror shattering on the ground. He is now trying to put the shattered pieces back together, to become whole once again, to heal. I shall call my friend XYZ.

XYZ relayed to me the story of events that led him to where I found him hiding from the world, weeping. XWZ told me of massive mood swings, from crying to rage. At one point, XYZ put his hands around another's throat and fought the urge to squeeze, and in another incident my friend contemplated ending their own life. XYZ wandered around aimlessly, ate poorly, and did not sleep well for almost three years. But, something magnificent happened to XYZ. With his emotions in utter turmoil and his life in almost uncontrollable chaos, he grabbed hold of himself and dared to look at why or how this happened. He looked at where he was and what had occurred. He found he was and had been—living an almost-dual existence. Over a long period, stress had built up and literally blown the lid of my friend's self-control and coping devices. This was not the first time, just the time it got beyond their control. And so the journey begins.

XYZ is a very nice person; he is warm, giving, honest, truthful, and loving. During the journey he made to discover how and why this had happened to him, XYZ began to unravel a string of events that led to the shattering of a life. XYZ was publicly embarrassed, often by his father. Emotional abuse took place in the home throughout his life. XYZ's siblings joined in on the torment, and all refuges were gone. Coping was accomplished by privacy, being alone to enjoy a world of no emotional pain, a world in which they were safe, warm, and of value. From this world, XYZ developed skills in the arts and communication. From reading and listening to music, he moved on to become artistic, verbal, and very sociable. This gave XYZ the power to move out once more into the world around them, and did well. The problem was the demons were with XYZ; they had not been dealt with, just held in control. From the emotional traumas of his youth, XYZ felt anger, despair, loneliness, and no self-worth; he was told he was a failure. The mistake XYZ had made was taking these demons on as their own. They were not. These things—these events—were not XYZ's doing or fault. They were the fault and doing of others, therefore their responsibility, not XYZ's. But ignorant to this, XYZ grew and experienced life with all its stresses. As he journeyed back, he noticed patterns, patterns of failure.

As XYZ moved into the world, friendships were made, but they always ended in emotional pain. When he looked at this, it was not entirely the fault of these other people. XYZ had begun a pattern of behavior, a road to self-destruction.

XYZ longed for a loving, caring, and warm family that had only existed in his fantasy world. Raised the way he was with emotional abuse, destruction of self and worth—he was unconsciously drawn to the same kind of life. He began to behave in ways that would drive away anyone who was nice to them. In his mind, being nice meant he was going to be hurt by that person. XYZ's conclusion: emotional abuse is going to happen to me, so drive away those who are nice before they can hurt you. Instead, XYZ would befriend those who abused him emotionally; he would stay at jobs where emotional abuse was heaped upon him by bosses or co-workers. After a time, he would react by quitting the job, running away. He would search for the coping mechanism of his youth: the room, the private world, the control. But now it was complicated.

XYZ had married and had a family; he thought he did not have his private room. Trying to be the opposite of his parents, XYZ almost suffocated his family by being there. He would not leave the home; he had no contacts or friends who were his alone. XYZ encouraged his family to be independent, to be strong-willed, but did nothing for himself. One day he awoke to find loneliness within his family. All of the members had friends, associates, hobbies, and a life. XYZ had unconsciously made his home the child's room. The fantasy world of youth became the computer. XYZ withdrew from the family without even noticing they were. There was more trouble building for XYZ, and he did not see it either.

The world of work had become a macabre dance of success and sabotage. When XYZ would begin to do well at anything, he would do something to shoot himself in the foot. There were several small breakdowns that XYZ ignored. The ignored panic attacks; the ignored wide and wild mood swings. He self-destructed and made himself unwelcome and unwanted as a worker. Then more was added to XYZ's woes. XYZ had begun to seek what he had never had: unconditional love. XYZ began to become very enamored with the opposite sex. He had many liaisons and encounters; his ability in this world became almost addictive. The pattern was set once again. As in his youth, XYZ ran towards sexual encounters that had always given him satisfaction and what he perceived as love. For XYZ, the intimacy of the sexual relationship became confused with love. These patterns of behavior added more and more stress to XYZ, and the lid had come off many times, but the final one almost did him in. XYZ was married with children, their behavior patterns were causing a lot of stress in their family, and it exploded upon him.

XYZ found himself alone, friendless, and without what he cherished most: a loving relationship. XYZ's final meltdown had cost him everything, and he stood alone with nothing.

Despair washed over XZY like a tidal wave. He reacted with countless forays into meaningless relationships; he ignored work.

XYZ threw the artistic, kind, honest, and caring person away; he became the opposite, a closed off, selfish, dishonest, prolific liar. This set up the internal battle, as XYZ said to me, "My fight against myself." We all have many faucets to our personality. We have the ability to be honest or lie, to do good or bad. What happened to XYZ was that, as the stress grew and grew, they struggled with their two halves, so to speak: the part that said do unto others before they stick it to you, and the caring, gentle side that was giving and loving. We need all aspects of our personality, but XYZ's had become polarized at two opposite extremes. This was why their behavior had become so maladjusted to their environment of family, work, friends, and lovers. It was here at the bottom that XYZ had an epiphany, an insight into themselves. He sought professional help to finally deal with his demons, his stress. He began to pick up the shards of himself. How is XYZ?

Last time I met XYZ, he was still shaky, alone, and weak in such areas as emotional conflicts. But he is trying. XYZ has thrown off many chains and dared to step out into not just the world, but his world. He has begun to take his sanctuary with him into the real world. He is in command, he is worth something, and he is valuable. He now feels he is important and worth loving and being loved. The journey is far from over, and the cost has been high for XYZ. He asked me to write about this so others could read the tale in the hope that any signs or symptoms that seem familiar will be looked at. As XYZ stated to me, "Don't wait until you are lying in the gutter to realize you need help. The cost can be everything you hold dear, including life itself."

This is what one interpretive definition of a nervous breakdown is

A psychiatric disorder, usually caused by intense stress or anxiety, in which somebody becomes incapable of coping with daily life and exhibits low self-esteem or depression A severe or incapacitating emotional disorder, especially when occurring suddenly and marked by depression. *(This is from an Internet site concerning nervous breakdowns. For a more comprehensive description I would recommend using DSM-IV, the diagnostic manual for psychiatric and psychological disorders). Further, I would highly recommend talking with a professional in psychiatry, psychology, or your medical doctor.*

<u>Causes can be</u>

chronic and unresolved grief

chronic insomnia and other sleep disorders

unemployment

serious or chronic illness of a family member

academic problems

divorce

career burnout

death of a family member

social stress

pregnancy

deception by a loved one

<u>Symptoms</u>

little interest or pleasure in doing things nearly every day for two
weeks; feeling down, depressed, or hopeless

sleep disturbance nearly every day for at least two weeks

low self-esteem nearly every day for two weeks

inattention to personal hygiene

sensitivity to noise

physical aches and pains, and the belief these may be signs of
serious illness

fear of going mad

change in perception of time

periods of sobbing

possible behavioral changes such as aggression and/or irritability loss of appetite

recurrent nightmares

learning or memory problems where none existed before

significant behavioral changes such as withdrawal, social isolation,
    and aggression

Author's note: This is a serious condition and should be dealt with by professionals who have knowledge and experience with human behavior, medical and psychological disorders.

We Are Inside Out

I am almost where I have to be. For years I have struggled with something or searched for something. The last two years I have been on a roller coaster of self-discovery, a ride that excites, frightens, and makes you ill. I am almost at the bottom, almost losing all, almost face to face with my greatest fears: being alone, being unwanted, and living in poverty. Some people would slip further into the blackness of oblivion, some crawl toward the new, driven by something that some seem to have lost a long time ago. What seems to have been lost is that little inner voice we had as children, the curious, adventurous, and trusting spirit of a child.

Each of us will end up alone, unwanted, and in poverty. We spend our entire existence alone, trapped in our container of flesh. We do not let others touch our inner spirit, not after the first injury, the first love gone bad, the first emotional bleeder. We become unwanted by others who have been hurt; their spirit shuns ours. If your inner spirit still sings, the logical mind of others keeps you separate from them. I fear poverty, but what is poverty? We worry about material things, these things we cannot have forever, but merely rent them, or use them up. Real poverty is the loss of your inner voice, your guide.

This inner spirit is the one that opened youthful eyes, bright in anticipation of yet another day of life. This same spirit gently closes those eyes at night for a restful, peaceful time of dreams that refresh the spirit, preparing you for another day. Each day at work or play, you are at peace, your face is relaxed, and your eyes shine; your being seems to beam. Your inside is now outside. The inside spirit of others can now be touched. A smile from you, a kind word or gesture, even in the midst of adversity, brings hope and the warmth of true love as the two spirits greet one another. Your spirit has touched the spirit of another, a sensual and cosmic communication between souls. This is as when you were young: honest, caring affection given freely. Work and play become one and the same because you approach them as such.

Many people approach work and play not only as separate entities, but with no inner spirit to guide them. In a vain effort to fill some kind of void, many replace this empty feeling with chemical escapism or journeys of debauchery, lust, greed, or hatred. You were meant to wander, to investigate, to learn, to enjoy. You were meant to join your spirit to that of others, to exchange freely knowledge and ideas, and to join in the play that is true freedom. We are told we need, must do, and must have, by whom or what? Not from an inner spirit.

We do not need the million-dollar home, the two cars, the vacation, the boat, the bank account. We do not need the time-constrained lifestyle guided by success measured by material benchmarks. All we need is food and a warm dry place to rest. Why, then, must we struggle for these most two most basic of needs? We must struggle for our basic needs because of the false economic, social, and political ideologies of a people lost, lost and separated from their youthful guide, the inner spirit.

But every once in a while some discover their inner voice again. They smile, then quietly slip back inside their childlike life, where they dare to dream and wonder once more. We recognize them and will react depending on whether our outside is in, or our inside is out. To overcome poverty, want, desire, greed, and violence, we must recognize them for what they are. These human conditions and behaviors are the results of false ideologies, the offspring of a people who have grown old.

Old before their time to do so. Old because the inner voice is near death or deeply imprisoned within them. Old because they are outside in, the bright-eyed youth has been intimidated, bullied, or ridiculed into the prison of a false ideology called the good life. It is the good life for a dying people. The time has come to not stop the roller coaster, to not get off the roller coaster, but time to recognize the roller coaster. The roller coaster is a life guided by false ideologies, by false economies, toward an inevitable end. The end is the same for all the riders, even those who recognize the roller coaster. The difference is some of us are riding toward the end, not being taken for a ride.

Smoke and Mirrors,
Is There a Real China?

As many of my readers know, I have been in China for quite some time. It has been a valuable experience, as it was the real China, not the tour guide or *National Geographic* China. Now what on earth do I mean by that? Well, I got to work with, see, and deal with a large variety of Chinese people in their natural habitat, so to speak. They were not asked to perform, or paid, or threatened; they were themselves. Sounds ominous, doesn't it. Well, people, China is indeed the land of contradictions, and it is not Kansas, Toto. In China, you live like an outsider who has landed on the planet Mars. Cultural differences, yes, some, but not as many as you would think. Language barrier, oh yes, and translating into English just causes more problems. Now where should I begin this little exposé, this little look at something without wearing the rose-colored glasses. Let's start with who comes to China and why.

It seemed to me, the first type of person we would think of is the tourist. We travel to a land like China to see the history, the people, the culture, and the natural beauty. There are many, many tour companies with a wide variety in tour packages. This is a good and safe way to visit any foreign country. Just make sure you are with a reputable tour company; check it out. Ask other people who have gone to China. The tourist will see the China the Chinese want you to see: the buildings, the cultural shows, the food, and the people they select. It is part of China, and it is real, but only the smoke-and-mirror part. What about those who go to China to work?

Many foreigners go to China to work, not to set up a business or represent a large corporation, but to work. Working in China is safe and can be profitable, it can be an exciting adventure, stimulating, and sometimes a little scary. You really feel alive when you experience a country as a foreign resident. After some time, and when you feel more comfortable, you can travel around and experience the life of the people. Those you work for will of course do their best to look after you and protect you. They will take you on standard looky-loo tours—you know, the touristy thing. But you can do much on your own. I have several CDs of pictures that are both the real China and the tourist China. Find a few Chinese people you like and can talk with, at least a little, and you will be able to tour the back areas of China and see the real country and people. Don't forget the rich and powerful; you can meet them too if you are lucky. It is a valuable experience and well worth it. What of the corporate representatives?

Well, they get the business tourist tour, seeing just what the rep and the Chinese authorities want them to see. Is it good or bad?

Well, I am not a business expert, so how would I know? The bottom line is profit; if that is realized, it was a good thing. The business part of China is a whole adventure of its own. The kickback, bribe, and influence peddling are really alive and well in China. There is a dangerous twist: one phone call can put a lot of people in jail. No trial, no investigation, just jail. Remember that if you are thinking of doing business in China. Be careful and know who you are dealing with; there are some not so nice people there. Same as anywhere, right? Well maybe. Remember: when you think the deal is done, with the Chinese, it is not. They change contracts as they are being written or signed. Be sharp, be smart, and be aware. Always have your way out of the country close at hand. This is no joke, folks. It is real. So, where in this does the real China lie.

To some people, China is the world's largest commercial marketplace. There are over 1 billion people there, a lot of sales. It is also a third-world country when it comes to labor. Cheap labor and lots of it; why do you think many companies are heading there? You can maximize profits with cheap labor, low taxes, and no environmental regulations. China is a very polluted country, with little to no human rights. To protest in China is to risk your life and personal freedom. The Chinese nation put two men in space, but has no sewage treatment plants and uses human fecal material as fertilizer. It is not unusual to see people going to the bathroom on the street, and there is garbage on just about every street, even in Beijing. China is indeed a land of contrasts.

I look at China and the people like I do anything else: with both eyes open. China has a long and wonderful past, but it is the past. They are losing much of their history due to overdevelopment and pollution. The Chinese people are like everyone else in the world: some good, some bad, and some in the middle. The big difference is in their indoctrination. They are programmed from an early age; anything outside of China is not to be trusted and is not good. China is great, China is best. Sounds like the Americans, doesn't it? That is probably why these two countries eye each other as they do. It is OK to lie, cheat, and take advantage of foreigners because they have less status than the local dog in China. They look at you as not human. I found out what a visible minority goes through. I suffered from bigotry, prejudice, cruelty, and anger directed at me just because I was a white face, a ghost as they call us. The real China?

The real China is much like the United States of America, à la George Bush. Nothing outside of their own ideology of the world matters. Nothing outside of their own doctrines is important or truthful. They feel they have the destiny to rule the world and become the only race or people that matter. They are lied to by their governments and the party, but believe it all to be true. They watch filtered news and put on shows of patriotism. China is dangerous, as is the United States. The United States at least has the option of legally removing presidents. In China, the party rules; political leaders do as they are told or they are in disfavor. Do I lie? One thousand people were shot and killed because a government-backed developer wanted to build on their land. The army was told the people were revolting, and when the people shouted and waved their arms, the army fired. (This story was released to the world and can be found in CBC archives.) The people in China live in fear that, at any moment, their lives can be drastically changed by the party or government. The people will and do react en mass. I asked if China was beautiful, all yelled, "Yes, yes." When I questioned that the answer might be an opinion not fact, I was brought up to the school administration and told not to say such things again. From that moment on, I was watched and held in disfavor by all I worked with. They knew where I went, whom I talked to, and sometimes what we talked about. OK, OK, many governments do this, right? But I do not have to fear for my life in Canada just because I disagree with my government or ask why. The Chinese have a saying, "No why." That says it all.

A View From a Window

It is a cloudy muggy day outside my apartment; it adds to my somber mood. The past few months have been odd ones for me. Emotional roller coaster does not even begin to describe the concept. I sit in an environment completely alien to me, no communication available. I hear sounds and see people, but cannot be part of their social network. I perform my daily functions and return to my private world, or enforced exile. There are greetings, acts of social politeness, but no depth that reaches my inner being. It feels as if my soul has been cut off from me, and my emotions can only spin and bounce around inside the shell we call a body. In acts of self-preservation, I have struck out of my exile to embrace the world around me, but to no avail. It is impossible to break through the barriers of this alien environment. The second hand of my clock ticks relentlessly onward. Time—I have too much of it to fill. I see architectural structures, planted natural beauty, and hear silence. The only changes are the weather and the drones that are allowed to function five days a week within the environment. I seek rescue.

My head, heavy with emotion, dips toward the table, tears well up in the corners of my eyes. All is gone, all is out of reach. My heart beats within my chest, the function of which I no longer concern myself with. My lungs take in and expel air, their function of little value to me now. I stare with no emotion at my command. Fingers move, transmitting feelings to paper with no plan or outcome in mind. My eyes drift to the corner of the desk, to the piece of paper with those words on it. I stare at the words, hoping for emotion, but none to be had. I am not even allowed the emotion of anger at having no emotions. It is gone, gone forever. Pictures of the past course through my mind; tears well up in the corners of my eyes again. A smile comes to my lips as the first tear falls softly to my cheek. Warmth begins to glow in my face, and my eyes blur. They are gone and with them, me. A small voice in my head says with childlike innocence, *I am sorry.* Now the nose begins to itch as the tears well up more. My cheeks are stained with the salty water running down from my eyes. "It's OK," I whisper softly. It has to be OK or nothing we have done matters. "You are free. I am still a prisoner," I whisper. The smile on my face grows warmer. "I love you, I have always loved you," I whisper. "I will never forget you or my love for you," I say softly as I pick up that piece of paper. In my mind, I see a lone piper standing high on a hill; I hear the strains of "Amazing Grace" played to perfection. "We are sorry to inform you of the death of your father," the words on the paper state. I have two other pieces of paper with words that are similar. "We are sorry to inform you of the death of your mother," and, "We are sorry to inform you of the death of your brother." I am stung with guilt. I cannot even remember the dates of their deaths, but I can remember the date of their births and the life that intertwined with mine. So I lay the latest message of departure down and look out the window. Good-bye to my dear father, be at rest with my departed mother. May the two of you hold close to you the spirit of my beloved brother, and may someday we all be reunited.

The Day for Mothers

I have been reminded once more of yet another upcoming special day: Mother's Day. I am thankful I have some friends who know me well; otherwise I would forget most of these days. Oh I remember the big ones: Christmas, New Year's Day, but that's about it. I have even been known to forget my own birthday. I have asked myself why, as has many of my friends. My answer is that I have lost interest in the commercialization of emotions, devotions, and love. I don't need a special day to remember those important to me. Sorry, folks, you are not all on my Valentine's Day card list or my Christmas card list. Those who are have stood the test of time and the many trials of friendship. Now before you start yelling to have me boiled in oil for insensitivity, let me relate a tale to you. I do remember the spirit of these special days and, of course, my mother. It is with sadness that I remember my mother is no longer with us, but I smile and remember her as she was when she was alive. Being a father, I remember my wife, the mother of our children, on Mother's Day. I was a good father and reminded my children to get something for their mother on Mother's Day, at least until they left home. There are now old enough to be responsible for themselves. I remember my wife on Mother's Day for probably different reasons.

There were times when I had to take on mum's job so to speak. There were the times when my wife was in the hospital having our second or third child. Other times were when she was in the hospital for a medical condition. On these occasions, I would take my holidays and be at home with the children. I learned firsthand what she goes through day after day. There was, of course, the endless preparation of meals. It seemed I had just finished the dishes and the next meal was in need of preparation. This was broken up with picking up after, stopping one child from eliminating his or her sibling, and answering phone calls. Salespeople, relatives, friends; these always seemed to come when one child was about to destroy the kitchen, the other the bathroom, and the third had decided to run away from home—again. I learned quickly that being polite on the phone was not possible; my diplomacy skills were gone two hours after the children thundered into the kitchen. Of course, my children were too young at these stages to be in soccer, hockey, or any other extra activities we often force them into for our own good. (Sorry kids, we need a break from you, too.) My all-time favorite was doing the laundry, especially when some of my children were still in diapers. My initial response was to control my gag reflex, which took some time. Then lifting the diaper pail to take to the laundry just about pulled out my shoulder. (Yes, people, we washed diapers; we did not use disposables. Save the environment you know.)

After a very full day, and endless excuses, glasses of water, and bedtime stories, the children would go to sleep. Late into the night, I would fold the clothes, do the final picking up of items, and maybe, just maybe, get some time to myself. Usually it was to fall exhausted onto the bed and hope for a good night's sleep. I would need my strength to carry on the next day. So now, when Mother's Day comes, my mind reminds me of my experiences as a mom. Yes, ladies, I know I can't give birth, but I can experience the rest. So here's to all the mothers out there: you have the patience of saints, the drive of a superstar, the will of iron, and still find the time to take care of us guys. Thank you, Mum.

No, I Don't Want to Be a Writer!

Did you get any writing done? That question has been asked of me sometimes almost daily. I usually answer, "Nothing publishable." The writing of this article was inspired by that question and one I often hear: "So, you want to be a writer?" I thought about this and decided to tackle both the question and the statement in this article. I will try one at a time. I am getting older, as I am reminded by others, and multitasking may be too much for those of us with gray hair. So you want to be a writer? I believe the question should really be, "Why do you want to write?"

Everybody has a story to tell. We all have lived, worked, played, loved, and had the entire gambit of human experience. When you read books, watch movies, or see a stage play, that is all they are about: the human experience called life. All stories tell something about life, someone's, a group of people, or an entire civilization. Why do you want to write? Is it for therapeutic reasons, is it for historical reasons, is it for pleasure, or is it for money? Most writers write because they love it; they want to write. Some are storytellers, and they are a very valuable part of our society. Others want to raise awareness or speak out against injustice; they are the conscience of our society. There are many forms and styles of writing, some write technical concepts, others tourism and travel, and the list goes on and on. The answer to the question, "Why do you want to write?" is for you to figure out on a personal level. "Did you get any writing done today?" If you have decided to write something, now comes the hard part: the writing.

One of the best courses I took at university was called Learning to Write Without Teachers. The basic concept is to write, and write, and write, and write. When I told the professor I had nothing to write about, he replied, "Write that down." Keeping a journal or diary is a good way for a writer to practice, and put down ideas for later use. From there, ideas for stories, articles, even phrases will emerge to build your stories or pieces. It also serves as a way to train your mind and hands to get on with the task of putting ideas down on paper and in your word processor. There are, of course, many other things to be aware of when writing: the usages of the language you are writing in, who you are writing for, grammatical correctness (I hate that one), sentence structure, readability, and so on, and so on. But you can have all that done for you as well, or you can learn. Just write down what it is you want to write. After it is down and you read it over and change things, your other skills develop. It is the passion, or lack of it, that will determine if you wish to continue to write or not. We write every day, not as much as we speak, but we do. Everything from grocery lists to notes left for someone that we stick on the fridge. So we all have the ability to write; we are all writers. Yes, we write something down almost every day. If you are serious about writing, just do it. If you wish to fix it up for others to read, ask questions and search for answers. Most writers are more than willing to share their experiences and give you some advice. The Internet is loaded with publishers', editors', and writers' groups. Do not forget to look within your own community; you will be surprised what you find there. Here is a final thought or two on the topic of writing.

From me to you: I write for several reasons, and you can pick one if it fits you. I write to placate my ego. I am a teacher and can't break the habit of giving information. I like to make people think, laugh, and even get angry to prod their emotions, to remind them they are alive. Yes, yes, I am a very opinionated pain in the @#@& sometimes. I write for my own pleasure, my stories of murder, mystery, etc., bring me great joy. I write for therapeutic reasons. When something upsets me or bothers me, I write it down and keep writing until an answer comes through the jumbled words on paper. Like some of you reading this, I love to relax, so the hardest part for me as a writer is the discipline. Write, and write, and write. See, it works! My article is finished.

Spiral to Hell

I feel alone and abandoned this evening. I am in a land far from my own, far from my culture and my language. I am not understood, or I do not care to be. I am abused by predators of a lonely heart. I am abused by myself, blame, guilt, feelings of betrayal to my very soul. Why you ask? Well I could lay out all the sordid details I suppose, but why? It is after all a private hell. Escape? I cannot see one at the moment. Actions for self-preservation? Trying, the old ways are not what they used to be. Pain, pain of the heart, pain of the soul. Alone, never have I been this alone in my life. Spinning in circles, searching for the way out of my bowl of water. Time, time, too much time. Space, space, too much space. Fight, fight to find my center, my inner voice, my guidance. Fall, fall to my knees shaken and weakened to my innermost being. Scream: scream at the moon, the stars, and the universe. The noise proves I live still, I am here, take notice of me.

I called out, but no one hears. They looked at me as if I were a strange beast and scurried into the shadows. I flail about, reaching, hoping, grasping. I find a thin handhold and grasp it with desperation, only to have it break under the strain. Again and again the process is repeated, my hands hot and sticky with my own blood. I hear a voice beg for the peace of death; to my horror, I realize it is mine. Die, damn you, die! "No!" I scream back as the muck of despair threatens to cover me. I claw my way upward, spitting the foul muck from my mouth, retching from the stench it carries with it. Why, why? How could this happen? It was not supposed to happen. No, no as the slime of the beast scorches my being. I try to find a path up and out of my pit of horrors; I search for the handholds of faith, of hope, of anything but despair. Sorrow chokes my spirit; I feel it begin to waver under the weight of hopelessness. No! I will not give in, I will not allow it! A loud beastly laugh I hear. A voice snickers that it is too late for that now. "Damn you!" I scream back and push with legs that now burn and ache. "Damn you!" My arms, now wet with blood, my blood, begin to weaken and stiffen. Just one, just one word would have saved me, just one word. But no, the word did not come, only the laughter of the predators. The laughter in the knowledge that they have yet another victim in their grasp. They taunt, they jab, and they prepare to feast.

Pain, oh God I feel the pain! My heart is not racing; it should be. My lungs do not rise and fall to give me the life. "No," I mutter, "No, it cannot happen." "Why not?" the harsh hot voice asks with a taunting of evil. "You are special? Ha, you are pompous, you are vain, and you are mine now!" My head pounds, my temples pulse with agony. My mouth dries, my eyes waver in their clarity. "One, only one word!" I scream. "Only one word," that is all I asked. The stench, the slime, the muck: they begin to carry me downward. I have nothing left now, nothing. I slip and slip deeper and deeper into the black hole before me. "No," I whisper with raspy voice and aching lungs,

lungs that no longer work a heart that has stopped and forsaken the body. "No," I plead in a whisper. Why? Why did the word not come? What did I do that was so wrong? Eyes fog over, mouth fills with bitterness, soul begins to die, and the spirit is gone. "Oh God, I am so sorry." The words are barely audible as my being slips into a dark cold nothingness. "Sorry?" The hot breath in the place my spirit once lived. "Ha, you are sorry! When were you ever sorry you pompous, little weasel of a creature! You conceited, self-righteous imbecilic sack of flesh!" My mouth cannot move to answer, my throat closed with a slimy foulness of retched bile. I have lost, I have lost.

From the outside I watch now. I see life pass by, mine and others. I feel nothing, I am nothing. Cold, I am so cold. Eyes that do not blink, lungs that do not work, heart that lies motionless in my chest. I feel no pain, no despair, I feel nothing. I can no longer move my mouth to scream; it would do no good now anyway. Eyes dry and unmoving. Skin cold and taut. I cannot think, I cannot remember, I cannot feel. Drifting, drifting further and further away, away from the pictures, away from the inside. Black, I am surrounded by black. No sounds, nothing. I sense that my soul, my inner voice, my guidance, has gone. I am empty, I am spent. Nothing: no smells, nothing to see, nothing to feel, nothing to touch. No sounds. I am aware, aware of the nothingness, aware I am floating in the void of despair. No guidance, no self, nothing. The word? I can no longer say it, or think it. I cannot find it. The hot taunting voice is gone; not even evil to keep me company. I slip, I slip further and further away from everything. It takes me, it takes me. I …

The Candle Has Gone Out

Spring approaches, the time for renewal and birth, the time of hope and promise, the time for warmth, productivity. But I stare into the night sky with a heavy heart and saddened eyes. I am spent, finished, used up. The last battle has been fought, and I have been defeated. The battles have been many and hard, but always I won or at least had a draw. This time my pride has fallen and my heart has been pierced. This time my spirit lies slain upon the ground, trod upon by the future. The old allies have turned their backs on me; I stand alone, defeated and disgraced. Honor, my old shield, has finally been cracked and broken. The sword of purpose has fallen from my grasp, my arm laid open by the wounds of my attacker. Faith, the armor that protected me, has been pierced by mortal blows, and the life blood flows out from within. Hope, that which surrounded me and kept me strong lies tattered upon the battlefield, trod into the mud and blood of the fallen. I, on my knees, breathe slowly. My mind is at peace, my muscles relaxed. I accept the final blow to come. I am at peace in my final moments.

The light sound of footfalls and my executioner draws near. I do not raise my eyes; I know the face, for I have seen it many times before. I slowly rise to my feet; there is a little of my pride still alive within me. The weapon is drawn; a short sigh escapes from my executioner's mouth. I hear the voice say that they know this is wrong, but they have no choice. I ask about the others. My executioner remains silent, and I know they have all perished. "They were my children," I whisper. "They were my dreams. They were my life," I say softly as I sink back down to my knees. The blow is struck into my heart, "You are too old." As I fall into the mud of ages, I look up into the eyes of my executioner. The eyes of time weep. Behind him stand the victorious generals, greed, vanity, self-indulgence, and their commander in chief, selfishness. The army they command is young, so very young. As my eyes close for the last time, I wonder, *Why does their army wear blindfolds?*

The Angel at My Side

The idea of angels has been with us for quite some time. Most religions have some sort of reference to angels. There is, within this concept, the idea that angels can be guardians. The guardian angel is a spirit who protects and guides a particular person. The concept of tutelary angels and their hierarchy was extensively developed in Christianity in the 5th century. Do I believe in angels? First, remember that we can use the term *angelic*; a person may be angelic. That is a person who does good for others, teaches, guides, and helps without questions or the concept of a reward. I will relate my tale, and then you can decide what you believe in.

There are many terms in our English language we use to describe not only people, but particular classifications within a society. Such English words have changed over the years due to, one would hope, enlightenment. I refer in particular to terminologies we use to describe those among us that are not mentally within the statistically evaluated range of normal cognitive functioning. I am old enough to have heard many descriptive words referring to some of these classifications, some not very flattering. What bothered me with all of them was the coldness. To me, all the descriptive and clinical terminologies were referring to my brother, my real brother. Over the years, my brother's disorder was called Mongoloidism, Down syndrome, and trisomy 21. Descriptively, these individuals have low abilities in mental functioning, often speech problems, and are of a particular body form with some distinctive physical appearances. Why would I raise the question of a guardian angel?

I was raised primarily with my mentally challenged brother as my only sibling. I developed and grew up within the sphere of his influence, of his morality. My brother was very honest, trusting, and giving. Even when others physically or verbally attacked him or our family, he would not rise to anger. His statement was, "Don't worry, they are just being stupid." Not bad for a supposedly mentally challenged individual. Now, my brother did have a temper, of course, but he would rise to anger for what I would consider morally correct reasons. If he saw someone harm an animal, a child, or a woman, he would go to the rescue, using physical force if needed. As for all us males, well he did not like violence and would not tolerate us fighting either; he would try to stop it. I was not a good boy in my youth, but my attempts to get my brother to break down his moral code failed. He never stole, lied or did any thing morally reprehensible, no matter who tried to lead him into it. He was a moral rock, unyielding in his beliefs of right and wrong. Basically he lived the Golden Rule and followed the Ten Commandments every day. His fortitude in this area kept me out of serious trouble and shaped what I try to do each day. Unfortunately, I am not the rock he was. But, for the sake of his memory, I try. He taught me more than any religion or priest about what is good and what is not. Then there were the actual rescues.

My brother seemed to appear out of nowhere every time I needed him. My friends and I were playing in an old car body up on blocks. It fell, and I could not get out of the way; the car body pinned me from the waist down. My friends stood around like thunderstruck loons, watching me scream. From somewhere, my brother arrived, reached down, and lifted the car body. He turned to me and said, "Pull your legs out, idiot." After putting the car body back down, he simply walked back to whatever he had been doing. There was the time when a bully was terrorizing a friend and me. Again, from somewhere, my brother appeared. He asked the bully to let go of his brother. The bully used some foul language, but my brother did not get angry. For the second time, my brother asked the bully to release me. A second barrage of insults was his answer. Very calmly and deliberately, my brother struck the bully on the top of his head. The bully released me and ran away—very fast. My brother helped me up, looked at me, and walked away.

As for my teenage love life, my brother was once more the moral rock. If I was being frisky, he would appear from nowhere, place his hand on my shoulder, and say, "You do not treat ladies that way." It is important to note that my brother was not easy to understand; he had a speech problem. But each time he spoke to me after helping me or chastising me, he spoke perfectly. That is the only time. There was only one time my brother could not aid me. He was away and I had a terrible accident; I fell off a cliff and almost died. Each time something bad happened to me, my brother and I were separated by distance, we were not in the same area at the time.. When he could, I was rescued both physically and morally. My brother passed away, and on his headstone are the words, "One of God's Special Angels."

So yes, I believe in guardian angels, but then I was blessed with a brother that only knew love, not hatred.

It's a Buddy's World

Thank you for taking the time to read my thoughts and ideas. I hope you enjoyed the peek inside my world. I am not naïve, nor do I travel with blinders on, but I do believe in the basic goodness of my fellow human beings. I have not been able to cover all topics, but am working on a second book. If you would like your part of fame, give me a topic, and I will credit you in the next book. We share this planet, this life; if one of us succeeds, we all succeed. I am not complete without you, the readers and my fellow human beings. Take care of yourselves and smell the roses along your journey.

B.L.G.

Bud L. Gilham